Y0-ELM-204

ADULT QUARTERLY COMMENTARY

SPRING QUARTER 2023

MARCH • APRIL • MAY

DANIEL'S VISION OF CHANGE

BIBLE BASIS: Daniel 7:9–14

BIBLE TRUTH: God judges the just and the unjust.

MEMORY VERSE: "And there was given him dominion, and glory, and a kingdom, that all people, nations, and languages, should serve him: his dominion is an everlasting dominion, which shall not pass away, and his kingdom that which shall not be destroyed" (Daniel 7:14, KJV).

LESSON AIM: By the end of the lesson, we will: RECOGNIZE that God judges the just and the unjust; TRUST that He has a future in mind for His people; and COMMIT to godly living.

BACKGROUND SCRIPTURES: Daniel 7, KJV — Read and incorporate the insights gained from the Background Scriptures into your study of the lesson.

TEACHER PREPARATION

MATERIALS NEEDED: Bibles, (several different versions), Quarterly Commentary/Teacher Manual, Adult Quarterly, teaching resources such as charts, worksheets/handouts, paper, pens, and pencils.

OTHER MATERIALS NEEDED / TEACHER'S NOTES:

_____

_____

LESSON OVERVIEW

LIFE NEED FOR TODAY'S LESSON

To remember that God has a future in mind for His people.

BIBLE APPLICATION

To understand that God judges the just and the unjust.

BIBLE LEARNING

Daniel's vision gives hope that the future will be better than the past.

STUDENTS' RESPONSES

Students will plan to commit to godly living.

LESSON SCRIPTURE

DANIEL 7:9–14, KJV

9. I beheld till the thrones were cast down, and the Ancient of days did sit, whose garment was white as snow, and the hair of his head like the pure wool: his throne was like the fiery flame, and his wheels as burning fire.

10. A fiery stream issued and came forth from before him: thousand thousands ministered unto him, and ten thousand times ten thousand stood before him: the judgment was set, and the books were opened.

11. I beheld then because of the voice of the great words which the horn spake: I beheld

even till the beast was slain, and his body destroyed, and given to the burning flame.

12. As concerning the rest of the beasts, they had their dominion taken away: yet their lives were prolonged for a season and time.

13. I saw in the night visions, and, behold, one like the Son of man came with the clouds of heaven, and came to the Ancient of days, and they brought him near before him.

14. And there was given him dominion, and glory, and a kingdom, that all people, nations, and languages, should serve him: his dominion is an everlasting dominion, which shall not pass away, and his kingdom that which shall not be destroyed.

BIBLICAL DEFINITIONS

A. Horn (Daniel 7:11) *qeren* (Heb.)—Of an animal; metaphorically signifies strength and honor; symbolic use in visions for kings and kingdoms.
B. Beheld (vv. 9, 11) *chaza'* (Heb.)—Saw; or in a vision or dream, it means to witness.

LIGHT ON THE WORD

What do you do when your faith promotes you and then casts you headlong into trouble? If you asked Daniel, he'd tell you to keep being faithful. Because of his faithfulness and excellent character, Daniel was promoted in King Darius' court. His enemies devised a plan to get Daniel into trouble. When he chose to serve God anyway, he was thrown into a den with hungry and ferocious lions. His faith prevailed when God sent an angel to shut the lions' mouths.

Right before our lesson text, we find Daniel trying to rest after a draining night in the lions' den. He tossed and turned all evening with God-given dreams. In the lesson, we learn of these visions that speak of the Ancient of Days sitting on a throne, ruling eternally, and giving dominion and power to the Messiah.

In the verses following our lesson text, the vision is explained (**Daniel 7:21–27**). The horn of the beast that made war against the Saints was one of 10 kings who prevailed until the Ancient of Days came and judged against him in favor of the Saints. Daniel's prophecy was one of hope.

TEACHING THE BIBLE LESSON

LIFE NEED FOR TODAY'S LESSON

AIM: That your students will learn to recognize and trust God at work on behalf of His people.

INTRODUCTION

Daniel and the Ancient of Days

"Daniel" means "God is my judge." Nothing is known about his parents, but he appears to have been of royal descent (**Daniel 1:3**). He is kidnapped by the Babylonians and is trained for the king's service. When he refuses to defile himself with the king's foods, the king's men divinely support him—Daniel only eats fruits and vegetables, commonly known today as "the Daniel fast." He is gifted to interpret dreams and visions and is miraculously delivered from the lions' den for his faithfulness. His career spans about seventy years, giving a time frame for the book of 605–537 B.C.

The Aramaic words for "ancient" and "days" are translated as "aged" and "time." Together, they mean "lifetime" or "eternity." God, as judge, is called "the Ancient of Days," or "the Ancient One" because He is God from everlasting to everlasting, and His reign is forever. The title is listed only three times in the Bible (**Daniel 7:9, 13, 22**). This same vision of God as judge is also given to the Apostle John (**Revelation 20:11–15**).

BIBLE LEARNING

AIM: That your students will trust God and commit to godly living.

DANIEL THE DREAMER (Daniel 7:9–14)

Not only is the Book of Daniel referred to in the New Testament more than any other Old Testament book, it also has more fulfilled prophecies than any other. Daniel writes at the worst time in Israel's history. The Babylonians destroy the city of Jerusalem. They take the Israelites into captivity, and now errantly consider their gods superior because they are able to bring down Yahweh's famous temple. Because of Daniel, however, this soon will change. Daniel's words stand as a timeless beacon of God's sovereign justice, offering hope to all.

Daniel is taken hostage in 605 B.C., during the first of three major invasions of Palestine by Nebuchadnezzar, king of Babylon and is a captive until the first year of King Cyrus the Persian in 537 B.C. (**Daniel 1:21**). His prophetic ministry continued until the third year of Cyrus, in 535 B.C. (**Daniel 10:1**). Through a divinely gifted ability to interpret dreams, God gives Daniel favor, first with Nebuchadnezzar, then with Darius, the one who is tricked into throwing Daniel into the lions' den. His supernatural wisdom continued to earn him good fortune through the reign of Cyrus (**Daniel 6:28**). Now in the first year of King Belshazzar's reign (the last Babylonian ruler before Darius and Cyrus), our passage opens in the middle of a dream Daniel had that he wrote down when he awoke (**Daniel 7:1**). Because Daniel himself interprets the dream right after our passage, much of the guesswork is eliminated (**Daniel 7:16–27**). The overall flavor is typical of apocalyptic literature (warning about a disastrous future or outcome), similar to the Book of Revelation (compare with **Revelation 14:1–15**).

A Vision of Judgment (verses 9–12)

9 I beheld till the thrones were cast down, and the Ancient of days did sit, whose garment was white as snow, and the hair of his head like the pure wool: his throne was like the fiery flame, and his wheels as burning fire. 10 A fiery stream issued and came forth from before him: thousand thousands ministered unto him, and ten thousand times ten thousand stood before him: the judgment was set, and the books were opened. 11 I beheld then because of the voice of the great words which the horn spake: I beheld even till the beast was slain, and his body destroyed, and given to the burning flame. 12 As concerning the rest of the beasts, they had their dominion taken away: yet their lives were prolonged for a season and time.

"I beheld till the thrones were cast down, and the Ancient of days did sit" (**Daniel 7:9**). Into Daniel's vision appeared a great, flaming throne on flaming wheels—the judgment throne of God Himself, "the Ancient of days," which in Aramaic was literally the "Advanced of days." God sitting in judgment was a familiar Old Testament theme (see **1 Kings 22:19**). The phrase "Ancient of days" is only used three times in the Old Testament, all in the seventh chapter of Daniel (**7:9, 13, 22**). Perhaps he was tired after spending the night in the lions' den; he says he watched until all thrones were put in place. And, he continued to watch until the Ancient of Days sat down. The Ancient of Days characterizes God as a judge whose reign is eternal.

The Ancient of Days' appearance set Him apart from the others, as Daniel described His brilliant attire, wooly hair, throne of fire, and the thousands and thousands of people who stood before Him. Then, court opened and while in session, two books were opened (one a book of life and the other a book of judgment). The deeds of the dead were recorded in the books, and they would be judged according to the contents.

Daniel wrote that the fourth beast was "terrifying, frightening and very powerful. with

12

great iron teeth" (**7:7, NIV**). The intimidating beast had 10 horns. While Daniel was watching the court proceedings, a sound captured his attention. It was one of the beast's horns that "spoke boastfully" (**7:8, NIV**). The beast was destroyed for its defiance of heaven and burned in the burning flame of God's throne. Dominion was taken away from the other three beasts, but their lives were spared.

Matthew Henry's commentary states: "Perhaps [Daniel's vision] points at the destruction brought by the providence of God upon the empire of Syria, or that of Rome, for their tyrannizing over the people of God" (Matthew Henry's Commentary on the Whole Bible, Vol. IV—Isaiah to Malachi, 1072). Further, it is also believed that the fourth beast is likened to the Roman Empire's destruction after it began to persecute Christianity.

SEARCH THE SCRIPTURES

QUESTION 1

Who does Daniel see in his vision? GOD

The Ancient of Days   himself

LIGHT ON THE WORD

Vision of the Son of Man

"I saw in the night visions, and, behold, one like the Son of man came with the clouds of heaven, and came to the Ancient of days, and they brought him near before him" (**Daniel 7:13**). Daniel continues to watch the vision unfold and sees the Messiah, who in the text was called "one like the Son of man" because He was made in the likeness of a human (**Romans 8:3**) and was found in appearance as a man (**Philippians 2:8**). The Gospel of Mark frequently applies this phrase "Son of man" to Jesus (**Mark 2:10; 8:38; 14:62**). Seeing Christ as Son of man suggests His rulership on earth where He was given glory, dominion, and a kingdom (**Daniel 7:14**).

I. FUTURE HOPE FOR GOD'S PEOPLE (Daniel 7:13–14)

Daniel's vision brings comfort to Daniel and his friends, as it foreshadows the stripping away of power from the church's enemies and reveals that Jesus' dominion shall never pass away. The church will forever be victorious to the end of time.

A Vision of Hope (verses 13–14)

13 I saw in the night visions, and, behold, one like the Son of man came with the clouds of heaven, and came to the Ancient of days, and they brought him near before him. 14 And there was given him dominion, and glory, and a kingdom, that all people, nations, and languages, should serve him: his dominion is an everlasting dominion, which shall not pass away, and his kingdom that which shall not be destroyed.

Daniel sees Jesus in His glorified state, described in a verse quoted frequently in the New Testament. W. Sibley Towner calls verses 13 and 14 "the very heart of the book of Daniel itself" (Towner, 102). Unlike the beasts or horns representing earth's rulers, the heavenly ruler appears as a man, "as the heavenly Sovereign incarnate," in Archer's words. In the Aramaic, the phrase "Son of man" refers prophetically to Jesus. Jesus confirmed this phrase as a description of Himself, personally claiming Daniel's words (see **Matthew 8:20; Luke 9:58**). Archer writes that Jesus regarded **Daniel 7:13** as an early indication of who He was (Daniel—Minor Prophets, 90). Jesus also used the exact same language as Daniel for His future return to earth: "they shall see the Son of man coming in the clouds of heaven with power and great glory" (**Matthew 24:30**); "Hereafter shall ye see the Son of man sitting on the right hand of power, and coming in the clouds of heaven" (**Matthew 26:64**); "And then shall they see the Son of man coming in the clouds with great power and glory" (**Mark 13:26**). As well, the Apostle John wrote in Revelation 1:7, "Behold, he cometh with clouds." The Old Testament uses similar language with God having "appeared in the cloud" on Mt. Sinai (**Exodus 16:10**), and He "maketh the clouds his chariot" (**Psalm 104:3**). Also, "the LORD rideth upon a swift cloud" (**Isaiah 19:1**), and "the clouds are the dust of his feet" (**Nahum 1:3**).

Jesus is given authority, glory, and sovereign power, similar to His own final words on earth just preceding the Great Commission, "All power is given unto me in heaven and in earth" (**Matthew 28:18**). **There are three terms in Aramaic that mean dominion or sovereignty (see Daniel 4:3, 22; 6:26; 7:27**); honor or esteem (used only here in the sense of heavenly glory, not humankind's glory); and royalty, reign, kingship, or kingdom (see **Daniel 2:44; 4:34; 6:26**). Here Jesus begins His earthly kingdom and all people will worship and serve Him— "every knee shall bow, every tongue shall swear (confess)," as prophesied by Isaiah (**Isaiah 45:23**; see also New Testament references to the same, **Romans 14:11; Philippians 2:10**). Unlike every manmade kingdom and empire, Jesus' kingdom and His dominion will be eternal, never to be destroyed.

When seen through the lens of New Testament eschatology (end-time prophecies), the little horn of Daniel's vision is commonly understood to be the "son of perdition" or the antichrist of **2 Thessalonians 2:3–4**, who will appear just prior to the return of Christ. Thankfully, we have the comforting words of a prophet in exile, blessed and prospered by God to a position of great influence, similar to Joseph in ancient Egypt, whom God used to speak to all future generations of believers. Through His messenger, Daniel, God delivers a word of comfort and hope to all who have known affliction, to all who have been oppressed, and to all who have wondered if there is any justice in the world. To all who have labored tirelessly

in the Lord, to all who have shed blood, sweat, and tears in service of the kingdom, Daniel reminds us that our God is still on the throne; He will judge the wicked, and the enemy will be destroyed, never to rise again.

QUESTION 2

What did the Ancient of Days give the Son of Man? RULERSHIP OH EARTH, GLORY

Dominion, and glory, and a kingdom, that all people, nations, and languages, should serve him.

BIBLE APPLICATION

AIM: That your students take comfort in knowing that our God reigns.

End of Days

No matter how long, vivid, and disturbing Daniel's vision was, he refused to turn away. He later wrote, "the visions of my head troubled me" (**Daniel 7:15**). What do you think kept Daniel watching? Was it nosiness, conviction, or compulsion? What can we learn from Daniel, as many of us find it hard to watch our own lives unfold? Many closed their eyes to our country's ongoing wars. They refused to watch the downward spiral of families, marriages, and economy. **First Peter 4:7** advises us, "But the end of all things is at hand: be ye therefore sober, and watch unto prayer." How can we take heed to his warning?

STUDENTS' RESPONSES

AIM: That your students will seek God to help them deal with tough situations.

Is there something God has been trying to get you to see? This question is not hard to answer. Perhaps, He's trying to bring your attention to your children, finances, relationships, community, or your emotions. You won't quit getting frustrated about it until you deal with it. God wants to bring you victory in the matter, but He can't if you're pretending to be blind. This week, challenge yourself to take a good look at a situation that's troubling you, and ask God to help you deal with it.

PRAYER

Lord, thank You that in times of trouble we can place our trust in You. You are our hiding place and shelter in the time of storms. Thank You for the hope we have because our future is secure with You. Reveal to us any areas of our lives that do not line up with Your Word. May we be aware of situations You are using to get our attention to make a change or move in a different direction. In Jesus' name, we pray. Amen.

DIG A LITTLE DEEPER

This is the ending of Daniel's vision of six kingdoms: four earthly kingdoms, Satan's kingdom, and finally Christ's kingdom. Daniel sees the rise and fall of Babylonian, Persian, Greek, and Roman empires as well as the kingdom of Satan (Antichrist). Today's Scripture foretells the kingdom of Christ. Daniel's vision answers the prayer in Matthew 6:10, where we ask for the kingdom of heaven to exist on earth. When this prayer is answered, believers will experience eternal peace. This vision fulfills the Davidic covenant in 2 Samuel 7:13-16, where he promised the seed of David would reign forever. This final vision provides hope to the current exiled Israelites and to all believers today that the Messiah will reign. We should use troublesome times to reassure ourselves of God's promises and make ourselves aware of God's message to his followers. We pray as John wrote in Revelation 22:20, "even so come Lord Jesus."

HOW TO SAY IT

Yahweh. YAH-weh.

Nebuchadnezzar. neh-byoo-kuhd-NEHZ-er.

Belshazzar. behl-SHAZ-er.

PREPARE FOR NEXT SUNDAY

Read **Daniel 9:4b–14,** and study "Daniel's Prayer."

Sources

Archer, Gleason L., Jr. Daniel—Minor Prophets. The Expositor's Bible Commentary, vol. 7. Edited by Frank E. Gaebelein. Grand Rapids, MI: Zondervan, 1985. 88–91.

Better Days Are Coming.com. http://www.betterday- sarecoming.com (accessed April 11, 2011).

Biblical Words Pronunciation Guide. http://netminis- tries.org/Bbasics/bwords.htm (accessed November 3, 2011).

Bullock, C. Hassell. Introduction to the Old Testament Prophetic Books. Chicago, IL: Moody Press, 1986. 279–300.

Hartman, Louis F. Anchor Bible, the Book of Daniel. Versions. Blue Letter Bible.org. http://www.bluelet- terbible.org/ (accessed March 29, 2011).

Old Testament Hebrew Lexicon. http://www.biblestu- dytools.com/lexicons/hebrew (accessed October 29, 2011).

Smith, William. Smith's Bible Dictionary. Peabody, MA: Hendrickson Publishers, 2000. 135, 201.

Strong, James. Strong's Concordance with Hebrew and Greek Lexicon. http://www.eliyah.com/lexicon. html (accessed May 1-5, 2011).

Towner, W. Sibley. Daniel. Interpretation: A Bible Com- mentary for Teaching and Preaching. Atlanta, GA: John Knox Press, 1984. 96–104.

Word in Life Study Bible (NKJV). Nashville, TN: Thomas Nelson Publishers, 1982.

DAILY HOME BIBLE READINGS

MONDAY
The Lord Deals with the Mighty
(Daniel 5:13–21)

TUESDAY
The Lord Judges the Powerful
(Daniel 5:22–31)

WEDNESDAY
The Plot to Undermine Daniel
(Daniel 6:1–10)

THURSDAY
The Plot Fails
(Daniel 6:11–23)

FRIDAY
Daniel's God Is Exalted
(Daniel 6:24–28)

SATURDAY
Daniel's Vision
(Daniel 7:1–8)

SUNDAY
The Exaltation of the Coming One
(Daniel 7:9–14)

DANIEL'S PRAYER

BIBLE BASIS: Daniel 9:4b–14

BIBLE TRUTH: God is merciful.

MEMORY VERSE: "To the Lord our God belong mercies and forgivenesses, though we have rebelled against him" (Daniel 9:9, KJV).

LESSON AIM: By the end of the lesson, we will: RECOGNIZE humans in fullness; TRUST that God forgives us of our sins; and CALL on God in times of great distress.

BACKGROUND SCRIPTURES: Daniel 9:3-19, KJV — Read and incorporate the insights gained from the Background Scriptures into your study of the lesson.

TEACHER PREPARATION

MATERIALS NEEDED: Bibles, (several different versions), Quarterly Commentary/Teacher Manual, Adult Quarterly, teaching resources such as charts, worksheets/handouts, paper, pens, and pencils.

OTHER MATERIALS NEEDED / TEACHER'S NOTES:

_____

_____

LESSON OVERVIEW

LIFE NEED FOR TODAY'S LESSON

To remember that God is merciful but we must go to Him to obtain mercy.

BIBLE APPLICATION

To begin to understand that God forgives when we humble ourselves.

BIBLE LEARNING

We must recognize human sinfulness and go to God for forgiveness.

STUDENTS' RESPONSES

Students will trust God's forgiveness and call on Him in times of great distress.

LESSON SCRIPTURE

DANIEL 9:4b–14, KJV

4b. O Lord, the great and dreadful God, keeping the covenant and mercy to them that love him, and to them that keep his commandments;

5. We have sinned, and have committed in- iquity, and have done wickedly, and have re- belled, even by departing from thy precepts and from thy judgments:

6. Neither have we hearkened unto thy ser- vants the prophets, which spake in thy name to our kings, our princes, and our fathers, and to all the people of the land.

7. O LORD, righteousness belongeth unto thee, but unto us confusion of faces, as at this day; to the men of Judah, and to the inhabitants of Jerusalem, and unto all Israel, that are near, and that are far off, through all the countries whither thou hast driven them, because of their trespass that they have trespassed against thee.

8. O Lord, to us belongeth confusion of face, to our kings, to our princes, and to our fathers, because we have sinned against thee.

9. To the Lord our God belong mercies and forgivenesses, though we have rebelled against him;

10. Neither have we obeyed the voice of the LORD our God, to walk in his laws, which he set before us by his servants the prophets.

11. Yea, all Israel have transgressed thy law, even by departing, that they might not obey thy voice; therefore the curse is poured upon us, and the oath that is written in the law of Moses the servant of God, because we have sinned against him.

12. And he hath confirmed his words, which he spake against us, and against our judges that judged us, by bringing upon us a great evil: for under the whole heaven hath not been done as hath been done upon Jerusalem.

13. As it is written in the law of Moses, all this evil is come upon us: yet made we not our prayer before the LORD our God, that we might turn from our iniquities, and understand thy truth.

14. Therefore hath the LORD watched upon the evil, and brought it upon us: for the LORD our God is righteous in all his works which he doeth: for we obeyed not his voice.

BIBLICAL DEFINITIONS

A. Trespass (Daniel 9:7) *ma'al* (Heb.)—To commit an unfaithful or treacherous act.
B. Transgress (v. 11) *'abar* (Heb.)—To go away or depart from the truth or way.

LIGHT ON THE WORD

Long before Isaiah and Jeremiah, when kings ruled Jerusalem, the Lord swore judgment upon His people for their wickedness. Manasseh, the son of King Hezekiah and king of Judah, was most wicked of all. He reigned longer than any other king in Judah's history—55 years of mixing faith in the Lord with idolatrous practices, placing heathen altars and images in the Temple, and sacrificing his own sons as burnt offerings to a pagan god (**2 Chronicles 33:2–9**). His son, Amon, reigned after him and did no better. But his grandson, Josiah, followed the Lord (**2 Kings 22:1–7**) and restored the Temple. Even as Josiah's repairs were being made, the Lord reiterated His intentions to allow Judah's captivity.

God's judgment came to pass during the Prophet Jeremiah's reign. The Babylonians attacked Jerusalem three times, finally destroying the city in 587 B.C. Throughout the attacks, Jeremiah continued to warn his people to turn back to God, give up their idols, and halt their alliances with foreign countries, but they ignored him. The people did not believe God would let them be captured by foreigners, and they did not think their Temple would ever be destroyed. They thought their covenant with God warranted them special protection, even though they did not honor it.

During Jerusalem's siege in 605 B.C., Daniel was deported to Babylon as a child. There he was placed in a reeducation program to prepare him for service in the very government that destroyed Jerusalem. Eventually, he became the most powerful Jew of the exile. In our lesson text, we find him praying for God to make good on His promise to deliver the Jews. This is the prayer of a true disciple. Daniel is a man of integrity whose life revolves around God and His Word. Even the Babylonians recognized Daniel's impeccable character when those closest to the king convinced Darius to throw Daniel to the lions— a plan that backfired and cost the plotters their lives (**6:6–24**).

TEACHING THE BIBLE LESSON

LIFE NEED FOR TODAY'S LESSON

AIM: That your students will learn to seek the Lord in prayer for themselves and on behalf of our nation.

INTRODUCTION

Captivity of the Jews

At the time of our text, the Jews were still being held captive by the Babylonians. Daniel foresees seventy weeks of desolation for Jerusalem, and he turns to God in prayer as he realizes that the time of the 70 years is drawing to a close. Daniel's prayer affirmed and endorsed the Prophet Jeremiah's words about seventy years of captivity for Israel (**Jeremiah 25:11–12; 29:10**). The length of the exile is also confirmed in **2 Chronicles 36:20–21**. Jeremiah had prophesied that after 70 years of Babylonian captivity, God would release the Jews. "For thus saith the LORD, That after seventy years be accomplished at Babylon I will visit you, and perform my good word toward you, in causing you to return to this place" (**Jeremiah 29:10**). In our lesson text, Daniel prays for God to remember to make good on His promise of deliverance.

BIBLE LEARNING

AIM: That your students will trust God to make good on His promises.

I. DANIEL'S PETITION FOR HIS NATION (Daniel 9:4b–8)

Daniel's response to Jeremiah's prophecy is interesting. Instead of concerning himself with the dates of expiration for Jerusalem's captivity, he was more concerned about the hearts of the people, and he repented for them. He could have taken Jeremiah's prophecy to King Darius and told him to let them go, or he could have simply waited, knowing they would go home soon. He simply remembered why they were captured in the first place and went to God on behalf of his people. Instead of focusing on when they would go home, he asked God if they were ready to go.

A Prayer of Confession (verses 4b–8)
4b O Lord, the great and dreadful God, keeping the covenant and mercy to them that love him, and to them that keep his commandments; 5 We have sinned, and have committed iniquity, and have done wickedly, and have rebelled, even by departing from thy precepts and from thy judgments: 6 Neither have we hearkened unto thy servants the prophets, which spake in thy name to our kings, our princes, and our fathers, and to all the people of the land. 7 O LORD, righteousness belongeth unto thee, but unto us confusion of faces, as at this day; to the men of Judah, and to the inhabitants of Jerusalem, and unto all Israel, that are near, and that are far off, through all the countries whither thou hast driven them, because of their trespass that they have trespassed against thee. 8 O Lord, to us belongeth confusion of face, to our kings, to our princes, and to our fathers, because we have sinned against thee.

In **verse 3**, Daniel writes, "I set my face unto the Lord God," which versions such as NKJV translate as "I turned my face"—a clear allusion to the Middle Eastern practice, still in effect, of turning toward Jerusalem to pray. Much Jewish and Christian architecture as well positioned the holiest part of their churches and synagogues facing toward Jerusalem. The first half of verse 4, which reads, "And I prayed unto the LORD my God, and made my confession," sets the tone for the whole prayer. This passage has been called "Daniel's Great Prayer," which continues to 9:19. Sibley Towner calls it a "great prose prayer of penitence" (**Daniel, 128**). Similar prayers can be found in **Ezra 9:6–15** and **Nehemiah 1:5–11**—just two examples among dozens in the Old Testament.

Also, in **Daniel 9:3**, he prepared himself for such a solemn prayer by fasting, mourning, and wearing sackcloth. He knew his prayer would not be based on Israel's merit, for their exile was a righteous judgment of their having utterly forsaken God. In today's language, one would say someone had worked very hard to earn such a harsh sentence, and deserved every bit of it and more. Israel's sins had included unrepentant idolatry, immorality, and martyrdom of prophets. Daniel knew that Israel's hope lay only in the mercy and grace of God, as he saw implicit in Isaiah and Jeremiah's prophecies.

The prayer starts with a common reference to "Lord" (Yehovah) which is God's proper name used over 6,000 times in the Old Testament. Daniel also invokes the less common reference of "God" (Elohiym), a plural masculine noun cited about 2,600 times in the Old Testament, which is used here and four more times in the studied portion (**9:8, 10, 13, 14**). Having clearly addressed the God of Israel and none other, Daniel further frames his salutation here by referencing God's transcendence ("great and dreadful God") as well as His grace ("keeping the covenant of mercy"). In so doing, he acknowledges God's unchanging, righteous character. Like a loving parent, God does not change His love for His children even when forced to discipline them. The implication, which the rest of the prayer makes clear, is that Daniel recognizes that God has not acted

unjustly by punishing Israel, and that they fully deserved their bitter exile.

As the people's representative, Daniel includes himself in the confession, which also has been called a model prayer of penitence (compare with similar words in Solomon's prayer dedicating the Temple in **1 Kings 8:47**). His dual reference to Israel's sin matches the prior dual reference to God in the salutation and acknowledgment of two aspects of God's character, which again is framed with a double reference to precepts and judgments. In **Daniel 9:5**, Israel's sin is both "iniquity" which can be translated perverse and perversion (see **Proverbs 12:8; Jeremiah 3:21**), and "wickedness," which also translates and infers guilt or condemnation (see **Job 10:2**, "Do not condemn me;" and **Psalm 94:21**, "condemn the innocent blood"). These great sins violated both "precepts," which can mean commandments, and "judgments," both of which refer equally to God's laws or prohibitions.

The polarized contrast could not be more complete: righteousness for God and shame for the Israelites. Israel's former respect had turned to derision (disdain, scorn, mockery); their former glory had been decimated. All they once had was now lost—they had lost their nation, the land God had given them by promise to their forefathers, and even their freedom and dignity. A popular saying calls for losers to "pay the piper," but the biblical version is "the wages of sin is death" (**Romans 6:23**).

SEARCH THE SCRIPTURES
QUESTION 1
Daniel prays on behalf of whom?

Himself and the children of Israel.

LIGHT ON THE WORD

Genuine Humility

Anybody else who was stripped from his royal home, thrown in a lions' den, and shown disturbing visions might be angry with God. But Daniel worshiped Him and acknowledged God for keeping His covenant with them, even when they departed from it.

Daniel was not general in his confession as some are who say, "Forgive me for what I did," or "Lord, you know my heart." Daniel specifically said, "We sinned and rebelled, we departed from thy precepts and judgments, and we did not hearken unto thy prophets" (**verse 5**, paraphrased). Then, he gave honor to whom it was due when he said, "To you belongs righteousness, and to us belongs confusion." In other words, he said, "You were right, God, and we were wrong."

II. TRUE CONFESSION (Daniel 9:9–14)

We can learn from Daniel by allowing our confessions to have a combination of the personal, reverential, direct, and congregational. The more we edify and exalt God, the smaller we should become. Our needs, desires, and thoughts should seem insignificant in the presence of a Holy God as we affirm our desire to repent.

A Prayer of Repentance (verses 9–14)

9 To the Lord our God belong mercies and forgivenesses, though we have rebelled against him; 10 Neither have we obeyed the voice of the LORD our God, to walk in his laws, which he set before us by his servants the prophets. 11 Yea, all Israel have transgressed thy law, even by departing, that they might not obey thy voice; therefore the curse is poured upon us, and the oath that is written in the law of Moses the servant of God, because we have sinned against him. 12 And he hath confirmed his words, which he spake against us, and against our judges that judged us, by bringing upon us a great evil: for under the whole heaven hath not been done as hath been done upon Jerusalem. 13 As it is written in the law of Moses, all this evil is come upon us: yet made we not our prayer before the LORD our God, that we might turn from our iniquities, and understand thy truth. 14 Therefore hath the LORD watched upon the evil, and brought it upon us: for the LORD our God is righteous in all his works which he doeth: for we obeyed not his voice.

The Hebrew word Daniel selected for "forgivenesses" in this verse, which can mean "pardon," is used only three times in the Old Testament (see **Nehemiah 9:17; Psalm 130:4**). In one sentence, **Daniel 9:9** captures the timeless problem of humanity since the "Fall": man sins, then repents at some point, and God in His mercy forgives—then the cycle repeats again, over and over, generation after generation, century after century. No matter how faithless man is, God remains true to Himself and is continuously faithful. No matter how utterly sinful man is, God's commitment to mercy and forgiveness for those who repent is everlasting. These verses capture God's nature and His relationship with His people, and provide a snapshot of the Gospel.

Their sins were undeniable and egregious. By flagrantly disobeying God and rejecting Him, they rejected the very mercy and grace which they so desperately needed and the benefits of God's covenant, too. Among the many benefits they abandoned when they turned their backs on God were His many promises, such as protection if they remained faithful, an abundance of provision, and the respect of other nations (see **Deuteronomy 28:7–10**). Towner notes, "this chapter is a meditation of Scripture upon earlier Scripture." (**Daniel, 129**). Readers of **Daniel 9**, particularly **verse 10**, will notice that its words and phrases are almost entirely found elsewhere in the Old Testament.

The Israelites were without excuse or defense. Daniel's humility was both apropos and accurate, for Israel's sins indeed were monumental. In truth, it is hard to imagine how they might have committed even more serious crimes against God—that He allowed the entire nation to be taken into captivity for what amounted to the lifespan of an average man (seventy years) was evidence of the extent of His displeasure with the people called by His name. Towner writes, "the calamity has taken place because God is consistent and faithful to his character as Righteous One" (**Daniel, 135**).

Being just, God will not overlook sins of such magnitude without compromising His own character and making all His prior warnings meaningless. What example would Israel then be to the world if they, in essence, could get away with such outrageous behavior?

Why would anyone trust in God's covenantal faithfulness if He didn't keep His promises of blessing and curses? No other people would have any reason whatsoever to repent or follow God, much less obey His commands and trust in His righteous judgment. In a real sense, as Archer states, "…all this served to vindicate the holiness and righteousness of God and to demonstrate to all the world the sanctity of his moral law" (**Daniel**—*Minor Prophets,* **110**).

Daniel's only recourse was to do exactly what he was doing, which was to throw the nation of Israel on the mercy of God's court of justice (compare with Moses' prayers after Israel's idolatry with the golden calf in **Exodus 32:11, 31–32**). Daniel appealed to God for the future of his people, his city, and his nation. Who would speak of God? Who would believe in Him if Israel were utterly destroyed and her city forgotten? This would be the greatest tragedy of all in Daniel's mind, as all the pagans from then

on would believe their gods had prevailed, that the God of the Israelites was weak because He couldn't even salvage His own people or protect His own Temple. Thus, Daniel leaned on the prophesied promises of restoration and pardon. As proof of Daniel's pure heart, God heard his prayer and responded through the angel Gabriel in the verses to come that their redemption already had been decreed (**Daniel 9:20–27**).

QUESTION 2

What did Daniel cite as the source to know their sins before God?

The law of Moses and the prophets.

BIBLE APPLICATION

AIM: That your students will not take God's mercy for granted, but quickly turn away from sin.

Holding out for God's Hope

God's dependable, steadfast love and mercy were well known (see **Exodus 34:6–7; Deuteronomy 7:9, 12; I Kings 8:23**). Just as Solomon prayed with faith in God's mercy, so Daniel held out hope for God to hear, forgive, and help (compare with **1 Kings 8:49–50**). Likewise today, regardless of the seemingly hopeless condition of the planet and its billions of people, every true believer can echo the prayers of the Saints of yesteryear, such as Daniel, who knew that no matter how bad things looked, faith and hope in God are always well placed and eventually will be rewarded. When all of this is cast as future, apocalyptic events, the historical principles become magnified but remain consistent—it is only through repentance that redemption comes, and this is because of God's perfect righteousness. Then, as now, as Towner words it, "God is called upon to glorify himself by saving a people in dire need" (**Daniel, 138**).

STUDENTS' RESPONSES

AIM: That your students will seek God in prayer and ask Him to reveal how they can please Him.

We can take God's kindness for weakness. When we mess up, we expect immediate consequences. If punishment doesn't come quickly, then we act like we've pulled one over on God. Many may continue sinning, as though God approves of their actions. How can we use today's lesson to teach those in our society who are stubborn, ignorant, complacent, or simply hard-headed that God sees all we do, and He will judge us according to our deeds?

How often do you confess your sins when you pray? Are you real with yourself about your deeds before God? This week, challenge yourself to go back to an elementary method of praying using the ACTS acronym. The letter A stands for "adoration." Begin your prayer like Daniel did—adoring God for who He is and the works He's done. C is for "confession." Specifically, confess sins of commission (things you did) and omission (things you were supposed to do and didn't). The T is for "thanksgiving." Thank God for His mercy, forgiveness, and all He's done and is doing in your life. Finally, the S is for "supplication," which means you make your requests known to God.

DIG A LITTLE DEEPER

Daniel's prayer opens with a review of God's plan for the captive Israelites as revealed by the Prophet Jeremiah. Daniel refers to the scroll as the Word of God. Even in captivity, God was fulfilling His Word as He will punish disobedience. Daniel's posture of prayer opens with preparing his heart and body for prayer through fasting, sackcloth, and ashes along with worship acknowledging the great and dreadful God. Daniel showed us how to approach God when we are found in sinfulness; that is, with humility and asking for forgiveness. Daniel entreated God to fulfill His word to restore the Israelites. Daniel also realizes that his prayer and intercession impacted the Israelites. Daniel lived a life dedicated to prayer, and thusly, he was prepared to hear revelation from God. As believers, our prayers impact those in our sphere of influence. Could it be, that the issues we are experiencing in our cities, our countries, and our world are existing because the believers have not interceded like Daniel? We encourage all to live a life of prayerful worship and intercession; the world depends on it.

PRAYER

Lord, have mercy on us. We do take Your mercy and grace for granted. Please forgive us; we thank You for the conviction of the Holy Spirit. We pray to live a life that pleases You. We pray for Your grace to make no provision for the flesh. Forgive our hidden faults, and use us to lovingly strengthen others. We pray for our nation, our communities, and our churches to exalt Your standards so that we may reap the blessing of Your power and presence. In Jesus' name we pray. Amen.

HOW TO SAY IT

Yehovah.	yeh-HO-va.
Elohiym.	el-o-HEEM.

DAILY HOME BIBLE READINGS

MONDAY
Daniel's Resolve
(Daniel 1:8–15)

TUESDAY
Daniel's Recognition
(Daniel 1:16–21)

WEDNESDAY
The King's Challenge
(Daniel 2:1–11)

THURSDAY
Daniel's Intervention
(Daniel 2:12–16)

FRIDAY
Daniel's Success
(Daniel 2:36–49)

SATURDAY
Daniel's Prayer of Supplication
(Daniel 9:15–19)

SUNDAY
Daniel's Prayer of Confession
(Daniel 9:4b–14)

PREPARE FOR NEXT SUNDAY

Read **Daniel 8:9-26,** and study "Gabriel's Interpretation."

Sources:

Archer, Gleason L., Jr. Daniel—Minor Prophets. The Expositor's Bible Commentary, vol. 7. Edited by Frank E. Gaebelein. Grand Rapids, MI: Zondervan, 1985. 106–110.

Bullock, C. Hassell. Introduction to the Old Testament Prophetic Books. Chicago, IL: Moody Press, 1986. 279–300.

Hartman, Louis F. Anchor Bible, the Book of Daniel.
New York, NY: Doubleday, 1978. 246–249.

Merriam-Webster Online Dictionary. http://www. merriam-webster.com (accessed November 3, 2011).

Old and New Testament Concordances, Lexicons, Dictionaries, Commentaries, Images, and Bible Ver- sions. Blue Letter Bible.org. http:// www.blueletter- bible.org/ (accessed March 29, 2011).

Old Testament Hebrew Lexicon. http://www.biblestu- dytools.com/lexicons/ hebrew (accessed October 29, 2011).

Towner, W. Sibley. Daniel. Interpretation: A Bible Commentary for Teaching and Preaching. Atlanta, GA:
John Knox Press, 1984. 130–140

COMMENTS / NOTES:

_____
_____
_____
_____
_____
_____
_____
_____
_____
_____
_____
_____
_____
_____
_____
_____
_____
_____
_____
_____
_____
_____
_____
_____
_____
_____
_____
_____
_____
_____
_____
_____
_____
_____
_____
_____
_____
_____
_____
_____
_____
_____

GABRIEL'S INTERPRETATION

BIBLE BASIS: Daniel 8:19–26

BIBLE TRUTH: God's promises give hope for a better tomorrow.

MEMORY VERSE: "And the vision of the evening and the morning which was told is true: wherefore shut thou up the vision; for it shall be for many days" (Daniel 8:26, KJV).

LESSON AIM: By the end of the lesson, we will: EXPLAIN why good decisions yield good outcomes; RECALL a time when we needed help from others; and VISUALIZE a better future in God.

BACKGROUND SCRIPTURES: Daniel 8, KJV — Read and incorporate the insights gained from the Background Scriptures into your study of the lesson.

TEACHER PREPARATION

MATERIALS NEEDED: Bibles, (several different versions), Quarterly Commentary/Teacher Manual, Adult Quarterly, teaching resources such as charts, worksheets/handouts, paper, pens, and pencils.

OTHER MATERIALS NEEDED / TEACHER'S NOTES:

_____

_____

LESSON OVERVIEW

LIFE NEED FOR TODAY'S LESSON

To observe how God uses others when we lack understanding.

BIBLE APPLICATION

To understand when we need help from others to make good decisions and to learn to ask for it.

BIBLE LEARNING

Good decisions, like knowing when to ask for help, yield good outcomes.

STUDENTS' RESPONSES

Students will plan to make good decisions by asking God for revelation and godly counsel.

LESSON SCRIPTURE

DANIEL 8:19–26, KJV

19. And he said, Behold, I will make thee know what shall be in the last end of the indignation: for at the time appointed the end shall be.

20. The ram which thou sawest having two horns are the kings of Media and Persia.

21. And the rough goat is the king of Grecia: and the great horn that is between his eyes is the first king.

22. Now that being broken, whereas four stood up for it, four kingdoms shall stand up out of the nation, but not in his power.

23. And in the latter time of their kingdom, when the transgressors are come to the full, a king of fierce countenance, and understanding dark sentences, shall stand up.

24. And his power shall be mighty, but not by his own power: and he shall destroy wonderfully, and shall prosper, and practise, and shall destroy the mighty and the holy people.

25. And through his policy also he shall cause craft to prosper in his hand; and he shall magnify himself in his heart, and by peace shall destroy many: he shall also stand up against the Prince of princes; but he shall be broken without hand.

26. And the vision of the evening and the morning which was told is true: wherefore shut thou up the vision; for it shall be for many days.

BIBLICAL DEFINITIONS

A. Indignation (Daniel 8:19) *za'am* (Heb.)—Anger, rage, or wrath.
B. Dark sentences (v. 23) *chiydah* (Heb.)—Enigmatic statement or question; perplexing statement.

LIGHT ON THE WORD

Two years earlier, in **chapter 7**, Daniel had a dream about four beasts. Now, in the third year of King Belshazzar (approximately 546 B.C.), in **chapter 8**, he had a vision. Both seem to predict future events, although some scholars believe the account was actually written after the events described. There is much, however, on which scholars agree. The essence of the vision is similar to the dream in that each involves mysterious animals, and in both instances the animals refer to kings or kingdoms of the world. Just prior to where our passage begins, three heavenly beings (two "holy ones" and Gabriel) are talking among themselves about the duration of the coming destruction (**verses 13–18**).

TEACHING THE BIBLE LESSON

LIFE NEED FOR TODAY'S LESSON

AIM: That your students will learn to seek the Lord in prayer and be alert to when He sends help.

INTRODUCTION

Gabriel and Media Persia

Gabriel was an angel who was sent by God to deliver messages. He is named in only four places in the KJV of Scripture (**Daniel 8:16; 9:21; Luke 1:19, 26**), and only Daniel names any angels in the Old Testament (see **Daniel 10:13, 21; 12:1**); Michael is named in the New Testament twice (**Jude 1:9; Revelation 12:7**). Gabriel announced the birth of John the Baptist to Zachariah and the birth of Jesus to Mary. In our text, he was sent to Daniel to explain his visions.

The ram in Daniel's vision represents the Medo-Persian Empire. Its two horns represent Kings Darius and Cyrus. The Persians overthrew Media under Cyrus in 558 B.C. and unlike other conquests, the Medes were appointed to stations of high honor and importance. The two nations seemed blended into one.

BIBLE LEARNING

AIM: God always gives you what is needed.

I. GABRIEL'S MESSAGE BRINGS CLARITY (Daniel 8:19–22)

Daniel fell on his face when Gabriel arrived, thinking his end had come. But, Gabriel stood him upright and explained that Daniel's vision foretold what should happen at the end times (eschatology) of the world. With Gabriel's help, Daniel understood that the vision was one of comfort to those who live in calamitous times, knowing that there should be an end to them.

25

God Sends Daniel the Help That He Needs (verses 19–22)

19 And he said, Behold, I will make thee know what shall be in the last end of the indignation: for at the time appointed the end shall be. 20 The ram which thou sawest having two horns are the kings of Media and Persia. 21 And the rough goat is the king of Grecia: and the great horn that is between his eyes is the first king. 22 Now that being broken, whereas four stood up for it, four kingdoms shall stand up out of the nation, but not in his power.

In **verse 16** just prior to our passage, Daniel hears but does not see God speaking with the "voice of a man" to the angel Gabriel in what is known as an epiphany, or a believed manifestation of the Divine or God. Daniel's natural response is to fall prostrate (**Daniel 8:17**), like John before Jesus in Revelation 1:17, but Gabriel prefers that he stand (**Daniel 8:18**). The entirety of our passage consists of Gabriel's message. His words "Understand. . . the vision" (**verse 17**), combined with "I will make thee know" in **verse 19**, indicate the importance of the messenger to communicate and for Daniel to grasp the message. While there are differences regarding the actual events referenced, commentators agree that these are future events (compare **verses 17, 19,** and **26**).

In **verse 19**, the term "the indignation" refers to Epiphanes' destruction of Jerusalem, the butchering of 80,000 Jews, and his vile desecration of the Temple, where he not only erected a statue of Zeus Olympios but sacrificed pigs on the holy altar. For Jews, all these acts were appalling, but none were such an abomination as the blasphemy in their Temple (see also **Daniel 8:13; 9:27; 11:31; 12:11**). **Psalm 78:1–4** seems to describe this destruction.

Regarding the "time appointed the end," this term in **Daniel 8:19** has generated perhaps more controversy than any other prophetic verse.

Hartman offers some tempering wisdom—that it "is used not in the eschatological sense, but in the general sense of any 'end'" (Anchor Bible, the Book of Daniel, 232). Compare with **Habakkuk 2:3; Daniel 10:14; 11:27, 35.**

Gabriel explained that the ram's two horns are the princes of Media and Persia. The horn that grew up first was shorter than the second one. The second and longest horn represented the kingdom of Persia, which rose last and was more eminent than Media. With its horns, the ram charged westward (toward Babylon, Syria, Greece, and Asia), northward (toward the Lydians, Armenians, and Scythians), and southward (toward Arabia, Ethiopia, and Egypt). The Persians launched attacks against all these nations to enlarge their dominion. The Persian Empire became so great that no one could withstand it, as the ram had in the vision.

The goat Daniel saw coming from the West represents Greece, and the horn between its eyes was Alexander the Great. In the vision, the goat did not touch the ground, and Gabriel explained that Alexander the Great had moved so lightly that he met with little or no opposition. In effect, he went to conquer the world. It is said that Alexander the Great pushed his conquests so fast and with so much fury that no one had courage enough to stand against him. He attacked Persia with three magnificent battles, killing more than 600,000 men and gaining absolute control of the Persian Empire. In the vision, the goat trampled the ram and broke its two horns.

Just as soon as the goat had become great, his horn broke and grew into four other horns. Alexander's kingdom divided itself into four parts—the kingdoms of Syria, Egypt, Asia, and Greece. But, a small horn grew out of the four, and became a persecutor of the church and the people of God.

SEARCH THE SCRIPTURES

QUESTION 1

What message did Gabriel bring to Daniel?

The end of days—"last end of the indignation: for at the time appointed the end shall be."

LIGHT ON THE WORD

Daniel's Vision Manifested in History

Just as Daniel's dream was interpreted (**7:16**), and so was his vision. Interestingly, the animals of **8:3** fit their roles in history. The two-horned ram (unified kingdoms of Media and Persia) was no match (**8:7**) for the one-horned he-goat (kingdom of the Greeks, led by Alexander the Great). As history informs us, Alexander's rise to world domination was meteoric but short-lived as, after only 13 years in power, he died prematurely from a fever at the age of 32. With Greece's goat king "broken" (**8:8, NKJV**), his four generals divided his kingdom, but none of them ever approached Alexander's greatness. These four were: Ptolemy Soter, who ruled Egypt; Cassander, who ruled Macedonia and Greece; Antigonus, who ruled Asia Minor; and Seleucus III, who ruled Syria, Babylonia, and the eastern kingdoms. Seleucus' son, Antiochus IV Epiphanes, headed south to Egypt and east to Persia; during his expansion, he also overtook Judea. Josephus records that it was in the 143rd year after Seleucus' reign in Syria, following Alexander's death, that Epiphanes entered and crushed Jerusalem, in 168–167 B.C.

II. GABRIEL'S MESSAGE OF THE END (Daniel 8:23–26)

It has been said that a statement is not true because it is in Scripture, but it is in Scripture because it is true. God's Word is the ultimate infallible truth. Notice, God told Habakkuk in a vision that justice, detailed in a series of woes, would happen at the appointed time (**Habakkuk 2:2–4**). In this sense, any future time appointed

by God could be an "end" (**Daniel 8:17**); therefore, certainly it would be true in the prophetic eschatological "end times" sense (see **Daniel 10:14** referring to "latter days;" also **Daniel 11:27, 35**). In fact, it is reasonable that we consider the visions of Daniel, Habakkuk, and others as verifiable descriptions of end times.

God Can and Does Interpret Dreams (verses 23–26)

23 And in the latter time of their kingdom, when the transgressors are come to the full, a king of fierce countenance, and understanding dark sentences, shall stand up. 24 And his power shall be mighty, but not by his own power: and he shall destroy wonderfully, and shall prosper, and practise, and shall destroy the mighty and the holy people. 25 And through his policy also he shall cause craft to prosper in his hand; and he shall magnify himself in his heart, and by peace shall destroy many: he shall also stand up against the Prince of princes; but he shall be broken without hand. 26 And the vision of the evening and the morning which was told is true: wherefore shut thou up the vision; for it shall be for many days.

Verses 23-25 describe the characteristics and the personality of the "small horn," which was Antiochus Epiphanes. According to Matthew Henry, Antiochus was considered small because he "was in his original contemptible; there were others between him and the kingdom, . . . and (he) had been for some time a hostage and prisoner at Rome, whence he made his escape, and, . . . got the kingdom" (Matthew Henry's Commentary on the Whole Bible, Vol. IV—Isaiah to Malachi, 1079). He seized Egypt, invaded Persia and Armenia, but ran roughshod over the Jews.

According to the vision, Antiochus set himself against God, heaven, and the church. He forbade the daily sacrifices and set his own image on the Temple. It was said he would be destroyed but not by hands. He would not die in war or be killed; he would be given over to the living God. And it was so. When the Jews cast Antiochus' image out of the Temple, he vowed to make Jerusalem a burial ground. No sooner had he spoken the words, than he was struck with an incurable disease. At first, he continued to threaten the Jews. However, as his illness grew worse, he tried to bargain with God to let the Jews worship freely. Finally, before his death, he submitted to God and wrote letters of apology for setting himself against the Lord.

Daniel was asked to seal the vision, for it would be more useful to us who live in the last days. New Testament believers are familiar with God's appointed times from incidents when Jesus told those He healed not to speak about it, for His time had not yet come (**John 7:6, 8**). Indeed, all believers today await the final appointed time when Jesus will return, something that will not be revealed to anyone prematurely (**Mark 13:32–33**). Demons, on the other hand, seem to be well aware that their time of judgment is coming, but it was not while Jesus was on the earth (**Matthew 8:29**). They also knew who Jesus was, but He did not permit them to speak out prior to God's timing (**Mark 1:34; Luke 4:41**).

Clearly, the time for God to open the seal after "many days" was in the distant future. Archer believes this "obviously refers to the crisis years [of Epiphanes' destruction and desecration] of 167–164 B.C." (*Daniel— Minor Prophets*, 105). The message was important enough to instruct Daniel to seal it up, to take measures to protect and preserve these words (compare with **12:9; Isaiah 8:16**). The great emotional strain and exhaustion Daniel experienced after receiving Gabriel's message about the coming tribulation (**Daniel 8:27**), prompted Daniel's great prayer of chapter 9 (see last week's lesson).

QUESTION 2

What did Gabriel instruct Daniel to do with the vision?

Shut it up [not to reveal it].

BIBLE APPLICATION

AIM: That your students will look to God for answers when their understanding is darkened.

Get an Understanding

At best, prophetic and apocalyptic literature is enigmatic to decipher— especially to assign to specific events in history or developing trends. Towner writes, "The concept of a predetermined historical sequence is one of the most difficult aspects of apocalyptic literature" (**Daniel, 121**). Sometimes it's hard to know what to expect when we are overwhelmed and confused. In today's lesson, we saw how Gabriel helped Daniel understand his vision.

STUDENTS' RESPONSES

AIM: That your students will seek God in prayer to make good decisions.

The plight of all cultures including African American communities are worsened when we make bad decisions or refuse to make decisions at all. Passivity robs us of opportunities to ensure a better future. Daniel being perplexed about the vision he saw, needed Gabriel to clear it up for him. What can we learn from today's lesson, and what we can do to ensure a better future for the residents of our communities? Go to God for the answers. He will give wisdom and reveal truth through His Word and often confirm this truth through circumstances or godly counsel.

Do you ask others for help, or do you try to work things out on your own? The person who does not ask for help is either prideful, suffering from low self-esteem, afraid of rejection, or a glutton for punishment. Asking for help is a sign of strength, not of weakness. Challenge yourself to ask someone to help you with a problem you've dealt with for too long. Consider seeking the counsel of your pastor, parents, financial advisor, friend, or licensed counselor.

PRAYER

Father, Your Word says if any man lacks wisdom let him ask for it and that You would give it to us liberally. You are a God who instructs, directs, and reveals truth by Your Holy Spirit. Help us to seek You for life's answers and be patient enough to wait on You. Give us understanding that we may be able to live according to Your will and by Your Word. In Jesus' name, we pray. Amen.

DIG A LITTLE DEEPER

Daniel's lifestyle of prayer prepared him to receive the revelation from the angel Gabriel regarding the end times for worldly kingdoms and the Antichrist. God wants His people to understand His message. "From Chapter 8 to the end of the Book of Daniel, the text is written in Hebrew, for the major emphasis of these chapters is God's plan for the nation of Israel in the end times" (Wiersbe, 286). God's Word comes for the benefit of His people. God loves us enough to send revelation of His Word through His messengers. We have to be like Daniel to not only hear the revelation but follow God's directions. Oftentimes we are not patient enough to wait for God's revelation and our desire for revelation is for self-gratification. Daniel inquired of God for the revelation of this prophecy (Daniel 8:15) because he wanted to inform his people about the work required of them. We see his true intent because after Gabriel told him the message, he also told him not to reveal the meaning at this time.

HOW TO SAY IT

Belshazzar.	behl-SHAZ-er.
Antiochus.	an-TAI-uh-kuhs.
Epiphanes.	eh-PIHF-uh-neez.
Maccabeus.	mak-uh-BEE-us.
Ptolemy.	TAH-luh-mee.
Seleucus.	seh-LOO-kuhs.
Nebuchadnezzar.	neh-byoo-kuhd-NEHZ-er.

DAILY HOME BIBLE READINGS

MONDAY
A Guide into the Future
(Exodus 23:20–25)

TUESDAY
A Messenger of Rebuke
(Judges 2:1–5)

WEDNESDAY
A Messenger with Good News
(Luke 1:8–20)

THURSDAY
A Messenger from God
(Luke 1:26–38)

FRIDAY
A Helper in Understanding
(Daniel 8:13–18)

SATURDAY
A Helper in Response to Prayer
(Daniel 9:20–27)

SUNDAY
A Helper in Facing the Future
(Daniel 8:19–26)

PREPARE FOR NEXT SUNDAY

Read—**Luke 22:14–30,** and study "The Lord's Supper."

Sources:

Archer, Gleason L., Jr. Daniel—Minor Prophets. The Expositor's Bible Commentary, vol. 7. Edited by Frank E. Gaebelein. Grand Rapids, MI: Zondervan, 1985. 102–105.

Biblical Words Pronunciation Guide. http://netminis- tries.org/Bbasics/bwords.htm (accessed November 3, 2011).

Ferguson, Sinclair B. Daniel. The Communicator's Commentary, vol. 19. Edited by Lloyd J. Ogilvie. Waco, TX: Word Books, 1988. 167–183.

Hartman, Louis F. Anchor Bible, The Book of Daniel.

New York, NY: Doubleday, 1978. 230–237.

Henry, Matthew. Matthew Henry's Commentary on the Whole Bible: Complete and Unabridged in One Volume. Peabody, MA: Hendrickson Publishers, 1991. 1127-1130.

bible.org/ (accessed April 16, 2011).

Old Testament Hebrew Lexicon. http://www.biblestu- dytools.com/lexicons/hebrew (accessed October 29, 2011).

Smith, William. Smith's Bible Dictionary. Peabody, MA: Hendrickson Publishers, 2000. 135, 201.

Towner, Sibley W. Daniel. Interpretation: A Bible Com- mentary for Teaching and Preaching. Atlanta, GA: John Knox Press, 1984. 115–127.

Strong, James. Strong's Concordance with Hebrew and Greek Lexicon. http://www.eliyah.com/lexicon. html (accessed May 1-5, 2011).

Word in Life Study Bible (NKJV). Nashville, TN: Thomas Nelson Publishers, 1982.

COMMENTS / NOTES:

LIVING WITH HOPE

BIBLE BASIS: 1 Thessalonians 4:13 - 5:11

BIBLE TRUTH: The Holy Spirit provides life-transforming power.

MEMORY VERSE: "For God hath not appointed us to wrath, but to obtain salvation by our Lord Jesus Christ." (1 Thessalonians 5:9, KJV).

LESSON AIM: By the end of the lesson, we will: UNDERSTAND the significance of the second coming of Christ; REJOICE in our salvation; and DETERMINE to be prepared for the return of our Lord.

BACKGROUND SCRIPTURES: 1 Thessalonians 4:13-5:11, KJV — Read and incorporate the insights gained from the Background Scriptures into your study of the lesson.

TEACHER PREPARATION

MATERIALS NEEDED: Bibles, (several different versions), Quarterly Commentary/Teacher Manual, Adult Quarterly, teaching resources such as charts, worksheets/handouts, paper, pens, and pencils.

OTHER MATERIALS NEEDED / TEACHER'S NOTES:

_____

_____

LESSON OVERVIEW

LIFE NEED FOR TODAY'S LESSON

Remember to offer hope to someone who is worried about the world or even this country—economically, socially, politically, and environmentally.

BIBLE LEARNING

Think of different ways to encourage people who need an uplifting word.

BIBLE APPLICATION

To understand the significance of the second coming of Christ.

STUDENTS' RESPONSES

Students will appreciate living a life that is pleasing before God.

LESSON SCRIPTURE

1 THESSALONIANS 4:13–5:11, KJV

13. But I would not have you to be ignorant, brethren, concerning them which are asleep, that ye sorrow not, even as others which have no hope.

14. For if we believe that Jesus died and rose again, even so them also which sleep in Jesus will God bring with him.

15. For this we say unto you by the word of the Lord, that we which are alive and remain

31

unto the coming of the Lord shall not prevent them which are asleep.

16. For the Lord himself shall descend from heaven with a shout, with the voice of the archangel, and with the trump of God: and the dead in Christ shall rise first:

17. Then we which are alive and remain shall be caught up together with them in the clouds, to meet the Lord in the air: and so shall we ever be with the Lord.

18. Wherefore comfort one another with these words.

5:1. But of the times and the seasons, brethren, ye have no need that I write unto you.

2. For yourselves know perfectly that the day of the Lord so cometh as a thief in the night.

3. For when they shall say, Peace and safety; then sudden destruction cometh upon them, as travail upon a woman with child; and they shall not escape.

4. But ye, brethren, are not in darkness, that that day should overtake you as a thief.

5. Ye are all the children of light, and the children of the day: we are not of the night, nor of darkness.

6. Therefore let us not sleep, as do others; but let us watch and be sober.

7. For they that sleep sleep in the night; and they that be drunken are drunken in the night.

8. But let us, who are of the day, be sober, putting on the breastplate of faith and love; and for an helmet, the hope of salvation.

9. For God hath not appointed us to wrath, but to obtain salvation by our Lord Jesus Christ,

10. Who died for us, that, whether we wake or sleep, we should live together with him.

11. Wherefore comfort yourselves together, and edify one another, even as also ye do.

BIBLICAL DEFINITIONS

A. Times (1 Thessalonians 5:1) *chronos* (Gk.)—A duration, which may be a point in time or a length of time.

B. Seasons (v. 1b) *kairos* (Gk.)—An opportune, set, or appointed time.

LIGHT ON THE WORD

Paul rejoiced with great joy that the Thessalonians had received the Gospel as the truth of God through the power of the Holy Spirit (**1 Thessalonians 1:5**). He then showed how deeply the Gospel's power is tied to those who proclaim and receive it, exclaiming, "So being affectionately desirous of you, we were willing to have imparted unto you, not the gospel of God only, but also our own souls" (2:8).

TEACHING THE BIBLE LESSON

LIFE NEED FOR TODAY'S LESSON

AIM: That your students will understand what Paul means by his initial use of the word "asleep" for believers in Christ.

INTRODUCTION
When Jesus Returns

The Thessalonians were enthusiastically anticipating the return of the Lord Jesus Christ. They were expecting Jesus to come any day and when some of them died before He returned, they wondered what would happen to those who had departed. They considered the return of Jesus in all His glory to be something that their departed brothers and sisters would not want to miss. So this is one issue that Paul is dealing with in the epistle to the Thessalonians.

BIBLE LEARNING

AIM: That your students will learn from Paul about the return of Christ.

I. THOSE WHO HAVE FALLEN ASLEEP (1 Thessalonians 4:13–18)

In this section, Paul corrected a misunderstanding about the return of Christ by the Thessalonian Christians. Apparently, at least some members of the Thessalonian church believed that only those Christians who were alive at the Second Coming would have the possibility of sharing in the kingdom of God at the time of Christ's return.

A Misunderstanding by the Thessalonians (verses 13–18)

13 But I would not have you to be ignorant, brethren, concerning them which are asleep, that ye sorrow not, even as others which have no hope. 14 For if we believe that Jesus died and rose again, even so them also which sleep in Jesus will God bring with him. 15 For this we say unto you by the word of the Lord, that we which are alive and remain unto the coming of the Lord shall not prevent them which are asleep. 16 For the Lord himself shall descend from heaven with a shout, with the voice of the archangel, and with the trump of God: and the dead in Christ shall rise first: 17 Then we which are alive and remain shall be caught up together with them in the clouds, to meet the Lord in the air: and so shall we ever be with the Lord. 18 Wherefore comfort one another with these words.

Paul referred to the dead euphemistically as "them which are asleep" (**4:14–15**). The point he made is that they are not dead and gone; rather, their bodies are asleep awaiting the Lord's call to get up. The Apostle Paul was anxious to assure the Thessalonians that once a person is saved, he or she can be present when Jesus comes again. Paul wanted to comfort his readers by assuring them that, in his words, Christians who are still alive "shall not prevent them which are asleep" (**verse 15**).

In **4:16**, Paul described Christ's return to Earth in a specific series of events. The Lord will descend from the heavens with a shout. The voice of the archangel and God's trumpet call will be heard. Christians will rise out of their graves and ascend into the air to meet Jesus (**1 Thessalonians 4:17**).

Only after the "dead in Christ" have left their graves will those who "are alive and remain" also ascend to meet Jesus in the air (**verses 16–17**). Paul appeared to have believed that he and many other Christians alive at the time of his writing would still be alive when Christ returns. Those who have ascended to be with Jesus will be with Him for all eternity when He returns to establish the kingdom of God.

SEARCH THE SCRIPTURES
QUESTION 1

How does Paul refer to believers who have died?

Asleep.

LIGHT ON THE WORD
A Question of Concern

The Thessalonians wanted to know if those who died before the Lord returns to establish His kingdom would miss out on that glorious event. The answer here is no. If we have already died, God will raise up our bodies into glorified bodies and take us along with Jesus as He returns for all the Christians on the earth.

II. THE DAY OF THE LORD (1 Thessalonians 5:1–3)

The Bible presents history as a process that will culminate in "the Day of the Lord" and this current age as the final moment before the intended climax (**1 Thessalonians 5:2**). John saw principles of evil at work that will be given full reign during the final moments of time. In the case of today's passage, the purpose of "that day" is to bring about the end of human history and begin the reign of Christ.

God's Wrath and Judgment (verses 1–3)

1 But of the times and the seasons, brethren, ye have no need that I write unto you. 2 For yourselves know perfectly that the day of the Lord so cometh as a thief in the night. 3 For when they shall say, Peace and safety; then sudden destruction cometh upon them, as travail upon a woman with child; and they shall not escape.

In talking about this anticipated day, Paul used the language of the parable found in **Luke 12:39** and **Matthew 24:43**, but he connected the "thief" not with Jesus directly but with "the Day of the Lord." This idea of the "Day" or "Day of the Lord," like many repeated themes in the Bible, can refer to more than one event—often even more than one event at once. This "Day" was greatly anticipated by God's people, Israel, for it held the promise that He would rescue them by destroying any and all enemies threatening to destroy them. But the prophets before the exile turned the phrase around so that on that day God would do the unthinkable and judge His own people for covenant breaking. This "Day" came about in 722 B.C. for the Northern Kingdom and 586 B.C. for the southern. Like many biblical images, the "Day of the Lord," has many fulfillments, but you might say, only one "Fulfillment," with a capital "F." So it is fitting that Paul, like Peter in **2 Peter 3:10**, joined together the awesome and terrible "Day of the Lord" with the long-awaited second coming of Christ.

QUESTION 2

The Lord will come like what "in the night?"

"As a thief in the night."

LIGHT ON THE WORD
Don't Speculate

Paul's vision here brought a revolution to the Thessalonians' thinking about the end: Don't speculate about the day or the hour, Paul counsels; rather, think on your standing, and the standing of the fallen world around you, since Christ will come as a reigning King.

III. CHILDREN OF THE DARKNESS vs. CHILDREN OF THE LIGHT (1 Thessalonians 5:4–6)

We now learn further why the believer in Christ can and should welcome the day of Christ's second coming: His identity is forever tied to the brightness of the day, and not the slumber of the night. By using the phrase "children of" to describe his hearers' relationship to "light" and "day," Paul used a common New Testament phrase to express an unmistakable quality about a person.

Unbelievers and True Believers (1 Thessalonians 5:4–6)

4 But ye, brethren, are not in darkness, that that day should overtake you as a thief. 5 Ye are all the children of light, and the children of the day: we are not of the night, nor of darkness. 6 Therefore let us not sleep, as do others; but let us watch and be sober.

Notice here that Paul was careful to point out the difference between the unbelieving world and true believers (**1 Thessalonians 5:3**). Paul described the unbelieving world as living in darkness, and believers as "children of the light" (**verse 5**). And "children of the day," i.e., believers, are not in the dark (unknowing, unable to perceive) when it comes to end-time events. We eagerly anticipate the return of Christ, and we live each day as though today will be the day. Unbelievers live as though they will never have to answer for their actions. Of them, Peter wrote: "In the last days scoffers will come, scoffing and following their own evil desires. They will say, 'Where is the promise of his coming? Ever since our ancestors died, everything goes on as it has since the beginning of creation'" (**2 Peter 3:3–4**).

Unlike those who are in darkness, "the children of the day" are awake, sensitive, alert, and prepared for that great and terrible day. Paul warned us that we must not allow anything in our lives that will deaden our moral alertness. When we allow sin in our lives, we soon become so overcome by its effects that we become oblivious to spiritual matters and unconcerned about the imminent return of Christ.

QUESTION 3

Paul admonishes believers to do what as they wait for Jesus' return?

Paul admonishes believers to "watch and be sober." He wants believers to be prepared for the second coming of Jesus Christ.

LIGHT ON THE WORD

The Christians' Identity

Some people have wrongly accused both the Bible and sound Christian teaching of becoming a motivation for laziness and complacency. They contend, if we remain in Him, our destiny as "children of light" is so secure, what motivation could we possibly have to live lives full of holiness and love? But this way of thinking is foreign to the Bible writers; without fail, they see the possession of Christ's glorious riches as nothing less than a call to action. This is why Paul began his charge to the Thessalonians in **verses 6–8** with the connector "therefore." The Christians' calling here lines up with their identity. If they are surrounded by the day and full of the light of Christ, then it makes no sense for them to sleep as if it were nighttime. Paul made it clear that there are "others" who sleep; those who have not believed the revelation of

Jesus in the Gospel are truly asleep with regard to the coming "Day of the Lord." However, it would be a strange and unnatural thing for those of the day to doze as if they could count on "peace and safety" apart from the love and mercy of Christ. Paul also rejects laziness and complacency by stating, "For even when we were with you, this we commanded you, that if any would not work, neither should he eat" (2 Thessalonians 3:10, KJV).

IV. WALKING IN READINESS (1 Thessalonians 5:7–11)

Just as he did in **4:18,** Paul reminded the Thessalonians that the uplifting truths of the Gospel are never just for their own encouragement. A major part of "watching" for the Lord's second coming to come is sharing with one another the hope and glory brought about by His first coming—His incarnation, death, resurrection, and ascension on our behalf.

The Hope of Salvation (verses 7–11)
7 For they that sleep sleep in the night; and they that be drunken are drunken in the night. 8 But let us, who are of the day, be sober, putting on the breastplate of faith and love; and for an helmet, the hope of salvation. 9 For God hath not appointed us to wrath, but to obtain salvation by our Lord Jesus Christ, 10 Who died for us, that, whether we wake or sleep, we should live together with him. 11 Wherefore comfort yourselves together, and edify one another, even as also ye do.

In contrast with **1 Thessalonians 5:7**, Paul sets up imagery of a soldier who is commanded to stay alert on his post. So must we as Christians. Paul instructed us to put on our Christian armor and prepare for combat. First, we put on the "breastplate of faith and love" (**verse 8**). The breastplate, a metal piece worn defensively, is to guard our hearts. Believers must not allow the world's situations to become issues that affect our hearts. No matter what the world throws at us, be it trouble, persecution, hardship, or even the threat of death; we are more than conquerors through Christ who loves us (see **Romans 8:35–37**).

Next, we put on the "helmet, the hope of salvation" or better yet, hope in our salvation (**1 Thessalonians 5:8**). Our hope is in Christ and His promise to never leave us or forsake us. People, institutions, and people all fail, but the salvation of Christ is guaranteed for eternity. God has not chosen His people "to suffer wrath but to receive salvation" through Christ who died to redeem us from God's wrath (**verses 9–10**).

QUESTION 4

Paul uses the image of what as "the hope of salvation?"

helmet

LIGHT ON THE WORD

Paul Reinforces Hope

Paul now reinforced Christians' hope in their ultimate destiny by explaining the loving purpose and happy result of Jesus' death in the place of His people. The words "wake or sleep" might bring some confusion. After all, has not Paul said that those who are "asleep" when Jesus comes back will find themselves in darkness and not in the light of His merciful presence? Indeed, if the word "sleep" here referred to such people, then the apostle would have contradicted himself. But Paul was actually looking back to an earlier use of the word "sleep"—found in **4:13–18,** meaning "dead." We know this because he was building on the comforting words of **5:9,** and because nowhere does Paul link Jesus' death with anyone's destruction. Jesus' death was only for redemption. Paul is once again encouraging the Thessalonian believers with the knowledge that both they (who were alive at the time) and their loved ones, who had died, will be with the Lord. When will they "come to life?" It will be at the promised resurrection of all people, at the coming of Christ "like a thief," as both **4:13–18** and our passage show.

BIBLE APPLICATION

AIM: That your students will begin to understand that there is a wonderful future with Christ after He returns.

Joyous Expectations

The people described in this verse were doing the opposite of "watching" and "being sober." By reminding the Thessalonians of such people, Paul strengthened his appeal that they follow a different course, in light of their beautifully distinct identity. As we consider this verse, it is important to keep our focus on the context of these commands, which is the hope-filled promise of Christ's return. You might say that the reigning Jesus will have one return, but that coming will be received in two different ways. To those in the day, those who are watching, the appearing will be gloriously happy. To those in the night, those sleeping, the appearing will be a terror-filled surprise.

STUDENTS' RESPONSES

AIM: That your students will know that the time and day of Jesus' return is not known, but it can be expected.

This week, ask a couple of non-believers what they consider to be the biggest worries of the country. Then, ask them how these issues affect them and their future. Use the response as a means of offering them the assurance of Christ.

PRAYER

Jesus, thank You for saving us and giving us the opportunity to love You and to know You. Bless us and remind us that we are to be prepared for Your return. Help us to share who You are with others so that they can experience the love of knowing You and being loved by You. In Jesus' name, we pray. Amen.

DIG A LITTLE DEEPER

In the Greek language, in which most of the New Testament was originally written, the word translated as hope is *elpis*, meaning "the happy anticipation of good" (*Vines Expository Dictionary of New Testament Words*, 1952, p. 232). The "good" spoken of by Paul in his letter to the church in Thessalonica is   the salvation promised when Jesus returns, resurrects the bodies of dead believers and takes them, along with those still alive, "to live together with him" in heaven (First Thessalonians 5:10 (KJV). Since this promise was made over 2,000 years ago and has yet to be fulfilled, and since Jesus Himself said even He doesn't know exactly when it will happen (Matthew 24:36, Mark 13:32, and Acts 1:7 KJV), how can 21st century believers do what Paul instructed the Thessalonians to do: live with hope by maintaining attitudes of thankfulness, patience, and love?

Modern science and technology have produced a previously unimagined pace of change and unprecedented wealth along with heightened human impatience, anxiety, and despair. This was illustrated when the corona virus pandemic broke out in 2020. It exposed the deadly results of the drastically widening gap between rich and poor and the already declining life expectancy of people in wealthy countries, such as the United States. It led to a deadly rise in automobile accidents caused by reckless driving and road rage, and dramatically higher rates of drug abuse, domestic violence, and other forms of crime – all providing clear evidence of the world's increasing darkness, produced because of disbelief in God and a misplaced faith in science, technology, and wealth.

How can Christians live with hope in these otherwise perilous times? The same way Paul advised the Thessalonians when he challenged the Roman Empire's claim that it alone could guarantee peace and security for those under its authority. Using Roman military imagery, Paul advised believers to put on the breastplate of faith and love that will guard their hearts and the helmet of hope – the hope of salvation – that will guard their minds (*Fortress Commentary*, p. 580) These elements – faith, hope, and love - shield believers from the temptation to go back to a life of darkness and from anxiety about how long it will be before Jesus returns. As a result, Christians can live with hope and happiness in any age and under any circumstances.

HOW TO SAY IT

Thessalonians.   theh-suh-LO-nih-uhnz.

DAILY HOME BIBLE READINGS

MONDAY
The Hopeless Human Situation
(Isaiah 59:9-15a)

TUESDAY
The Source of Hope
(Isaiah 59:15b-21)

WEDNESDAY
Waiting in Hope
(Psalm 38:9-15)

THURSDAY
Hoping against Hope
(Romans 4:16-25)

FRIDAY
Seizing the Hope Set before Us
(Hebrews 6:13-20)

SATURDAY
The God of Hope
(Romans 15:7-13)

SUNDAY
Encourage One Another with Hope
(1 Thessalonians 4:13-5:11)

PREPARE FOR NEXT SUNDAY

Read **2 Thessalonians 2:1-3, 9-17**, and study
"Hope Comes From God's Grace."

Sources:

Best, Ernest. The First and Second Epistles to the Thessalo- nians. Black's New Testament Commentaries. London, England: Adam and Charles Black, 1986. 205.

Biblical Words Pronunciation Guide. http://netministries. org/Bbasics/ bwords.htm (accessed November 3, 2011).

Henry, Matthew. Matthew Henry's Commentary on the Whole Bible. Vol. VI— Acts to Revelation. McLean, VA: MacDonald Publishing, nd. 788.

Keener, Craig. IVP Bible Background Commentary: New Testament. Downers Grove, IL: InterVarsity Press, 1993.

594. electronic edition (accessed September 2, 2008). New Testament Greek Lexicon. http://www.biblestudy-

tools.com/lexicons/greek (accessed October 31, 2011).

COMMENTS / NOTES:

THE LORD'S SUPPER (PALM SUNDAY)

BIBLE BASIS: Luke 22:14–30

BIBLE TRUTH: Jesus believed in service.

MEMORY VERSE: "But ye shall not be so: but he that is greatest among you, let him be as the younger; and he that is chief, as he that doth serve" (Luke 22:26, KJV).

LESSON AIM: By the end of the lesson, we will: RECOGNIZE that even Jesus believed in service; REFLECT on the sacrificial elements of the Lord's Supper; and SHARE the sacrifices of our Lord with others.

BACKGROUND SCRIPTURES: Luke 22:14–30 KJV — Read and incorporate the insights gained from the Background Scriptures into your study of the lesson.

TEACHER PREPARATION

MATERIALS NEEDED: Bibles, (several different versions), Quarterly Commentary/Teacher Manual, Adult Quarterly, teaching resources such as charts, worksheets/handouts, paper, pens, and pencils.

OTHER MATERIALS NEEDED / TEACHER'S NOTES:

_____

_____

LESSON OVERVIEW

LIFE NEED FOR TODAY'S LESSON

To observe the sacrificial elements of the Lord's Supper.

BIBLE LEARNING

Jesus says those who serve others will eat the bread and sip the wine at the table He has set for them in heaven.

BIBLE APPLICATION

To understand how we can better serve others.

STUDENTS' RESPONSES

Students will develop a plan to share our Lord's sacrifice with others.

LESSON SCRIPTURE

LUKE 22:14–30, KJV

14. And when the hour was come, he sat down, and the twelve apostles with him.

15. And he said unto them, With desire I have desired to eat this passover with you before I suffer:

16. For I say unto you, I will not any more eat thereof, until it be fulfilled in the kingdom of God.

17. And he took the cup, and gave thanks, and said, Take this, and divide it among yourselves:

18. For I say unto you, I will not drink of the fruit of the vine, until the kingdom of God shall come.

19. And he took bread, and gave thanks, and brake it, and gave unto them, saying, This is my body which is given for you: this do in remembrance of me.

20. Likewise also the cup after supper, saying, This cup is the new testament in my blood, which is shed for you.

21. But, behold, the hand of him that betrayeth me is with me on the table.

22. And truly the Son of man goeth, as it was determined: but woe unto that man by whom he is betrayed!

23. And they began to enquire among themselves, which of them it was that should do this thing.

24. And there was also a strife among them, which of them should be accounted the greatest.

25. And he said unto them, The kings of the Gentiles exercise lordship over them; and they that exercise authority upon them are called benefactors.

26. But ye shall not be so: but he that is greatest among you, let him be as the younger; and he that is chief, as he that doth serve.

27. For whether is greater, he that sitteth at meat, or he that serveth? is not he that sitteth at meat? but I am among you as he that serveth.

28. Ye are they which have continued with me in my temptations.

29. And I appoint unto you a kingdom, as my Father hath appointed unto me;

30. That ye may eat and drink at my table in my kingdom, and sit on thrones

BIBLICAL DEFINITIONS

A. Remembrance (Luke 22:19) *anamnesis* (Gk.)—A recollection.
B. Serve (v. 26) *diakoneo* (Gk.)—To be a servant, attendant.

LIGHT ON THE WORD

The Passover and Festival of Unleavened Bread were approaching. All Jewish males over the age of 12 had to go to Jerusalem, but the chief priests and scribes felt it would not be a good time to set in motion their plan to kill Jesus. They knew the large crowds that came for the Passover may rise up and stone them for hurting Jesus. So they tried to figure out how to kill Jesus in the most secretive way. However, they needed someone to help them do it. Satan entered Judas, and he consulted with them and agreed to betray Jesus for money (thirty pieces of silver) (**Luke 22:5**). He was just waiting for the right time. He went and joined the disciples, who were preparing for Passover in Bethany.

Jesus made preparations for Himself and the disciples to celebrate Passover in the upper room of a house. Peter and John went ahead to Jerusalem and prepared the meal for them to share.

TEACHING THE BIBLE LESSON

LIFE NEED FOR TODAY'S LESSON

AIM: That your students will describe to others the awe-inspiring preeminence of Jesus Christ.

INTRODUCTION

Holy City, Holy Memorial

Jerusalem was both the religious and the political seat of Palestine, and the place where the Messiah was expected to arrive. It is located 14 miles west of the Dead Sea, 33 miles east of the

Mediterranean. It is 3,800 feet above the level of the Dead Sea. The Temple was located there, and many Jewish families from all over the world traveled to Jerusalem during the important feasts. The Temple sat on a hill overlooking the city. Solomon had built the first Temple on this same site almost 1,000 years earlier (949 B.C.), but the Babylonians destroyed that Temple (**2 Kings 25**). The Temple was rebuilt in 515 B.C., and Herod the Great enlarged and remodeled it.

Jesus spent a lot of time in Jerusalem at the Temple teaching and preaching. Religious leaders often challenged His authority and teachings at the Temple. After the death and Resurrection of Christ, Jerusalem became the focal point for most events connected with Christianity, beginning with the day of Pentecost and including much of the history contained in the Acts of the Apostles. In A.D. 70, the Romans destroyed the Temple, the city, and its inhabitants with fire.

The Feast of the Unleavened Bread immediately followed the Passover and lasted seven days during the month of Nisan (March– April). On each of these days, after the morning sacrifice, a sacrifice in relation to the feast was presented. Unleavened bread alone was eaten and the Israelites removed all yeast from their homes (**Exodus 12:15–20; 13:6–8; Leviticus 23:6; Deuteronomy 16:3–8**). In the context of the exodus from Egypt, eating bread without yeast signified the haste of their preparation to depart. Moreover, yeast was not used in most grain offerings to God (**Leviticus 2:11**). Yeast can sometimes be viewed to symbolize sin. It grows in bread dough just as sin grows in life. A little yeast will affect the whole loaf, just as a little sin can destroy a whole life. A holy convocation and rest from work, with the exception of preparing food, were celebrated on the first and seventh days of the feast.

BIBLE LEARNING

AIM: That your students will reflect on the significance of the sacrificial elements of the Lord's Supper.

I. THE FEAST OF THE LORD (Luke 22:14–20)

The Passover meal began the Feast of Unleavened Bread. Peter and John secured a lamb, killed it, and prepared it for the Passover celebration. They also purchased unleavened bread, wine, and herbs. These were all necessary items for the meal. They made sure everything was ready for Jesus and the other disciples when they arrived from Bethany.

Institution of the Lord's Supper (verses 14–20)

14 And when the hour was come, he sat down, and the twelve apostles with him. 15 And he said unto them, With desire I have desired to eat this passover with you before I suffer: 16 For I say unto you, I will not any more eat thereof, until it be fulfilled in the kingdom of God. 17 And he took the cup, and gave thanks, and said, Take this, and divide it among yourselves: 18 For I say unto you, I will not drink of the fruit of the vine, until the kingdom of God shall come. 19 And he took bread, and gave thanks, and brake it, and gave unto them, saying, This is my body which is given for you: this do in remembrance of me. 20 Likewise also the cup after supper, saying, This cup is the new testament in my blood, which is shed for you.

The disciples were gathered in the guest chamber (also guest room or upper room) of a Jewish residence, the location of which Jesus had providentially selected.

Jesus' statement in **Luke 22:15**, "With desire I have desired," which is also translated "I have eagerly desired," emphasizes the depth of His feelings. It is reinforced twice with His strong words about never again eating the bread, and in verse 18 never again drinking from the cup, until some point in the future when all would be fulfilled in His coming kingdom. The synoptic parallels of verse 18, similar to **verse 16,** are found in **Matthew 26:29** and **Mark 14:25.** New Testament believers can still relate to the disciples in the Upper Room as we continue to this day to observe the Lord's Supper "until he comes" (see **1 Corinthians 11:26, NIV**). Jesus' enigmatic reference to the future kingdom soon was to become painfully clear to the disciples. Unlike any previous Passover, this time Jesus' body, the spotless and unblemished Lamb of God, would replace the traditional Passover lambs (**1 Corinthians 5:7**).

Luke differs from Mark in the number and order of cups. Commentators seem to agree that the use of more than one cup, here and in verse 20, both before and after the meal, indicate the standard Passover tradition that used four cups at specific times during the ceremony. The first cup is with the opening benediction; the second cup after explaining the Passover and singing the Hallel (**Psalm 113–114**); the third cup following the meal, which primarily consisted of unleavened bread (representing the Israelites' haste to leave Egypt), lamb (from which came the lamb's blood on the doorposts), and bitter herbs (representing the bitterness of slavery); and the fourth cup following the conclusion of the Hallel. Luke's passage records Jesus' taking the second and third cups before and after the meal, but not including either a benediction or singing.

Jesus' giving of thanks is in Walter Liefeld's words, "the source of the beautiful word Eucharist" (**Matthew, Mark, Luke, 1027**). Only Luke adds the words "given for you" for the bread, representing His body and "shed for you" for the wine representing His blood. (See also **John 6:11; Acts 27:35.**)

Unlike all other Passovers, with these words, Jesus ushers in the New Testament, the New Covenant, ratified in blood as were all covenants between God and men (**Exodus 24:8**). The word here translated "testament" can mean either testament or covenant (also an arrangement, compact, disposition, or will). Liefeld writes, "The new covenant' . . . carried with it the assurance of forgiveness through Jesus' blood shed on the cross and the inner work of the Holy Spirit in motivating us and enabling us to fulfill our covenantal responsibility" (**Matthew, Mark, Luke, 1027**).

Jesus is well aware of His mission on earth, and soon He will ask the Father to take the "cup" (of suffering) from Him if possible (see synoptic parallels in **Matthew 26:39; Mark 14:36; Luke 22:42**). Liefeld writes, "The suffering motif is consistent with Jesus' understanding of his mission as the Suffering Servant" (**Matthew, Mark, Luke, 1027**). (See also **Isaiah 53:11**).

SEARCH THE SCRIPTURES

QUESTION 1

What did the bread and wine represent at the Passover meal?

The body and blood of Jesus Christ.

LIGHT ON THE WORD

The Passover Lamb

It had been prophesied that Jesus, the Messiah, would be betrayed (**Psalm 41:9; Zechariah 11:12–13; Matthew 20:18; 26:20–25; Acts 1:16, 20**). The people had offered praises of "Hosanna, Blessed is he who comes in the name of the Lord!" as He entered Jerusalem riding on a donkey. Yet, they would eventually cry out for His crucifixion. In His death and shed blood, Jesus symbolizes the slain Passover Lamb.

II. DESTINY FULFILLED AT THE CROSS (Luke 22:21–23)

Jesus knew His destiny of death on the Cross was predetermined by His Father. It was not unexpected. Jesus had come into the world to save us from sin. This could only be accomplished through His death and resurrection. Satan used Judas to fulfill God's plans. (**Matthew 27:3–5**).

The Betrayal (verses 21–23)

21 But, behold, the hand of him that betrayeth me is with me on the table. 22 And truly the Son of man goeth, as it was determined: but woe unto that man by whom he is betrayed! 23 And they began to enquire among themselves, which of them it was that should do this thing.

After the Passover meal and Lord's Supper were over, Jesus said, "But, behold, the hand of him that betrayeth me is with me on the table. And truly the Son of man goeth, as it was determined: but woe unto that man by whom he is betrayed! And they began to inquire among themselves, which of them it was that should do this thing" (**vv. 21–23**). Here, Jesus let His disciples know that one amongst them, one who had celebrated Passover and the Lord's Supper at the table, had betrayed Him. The disciples became suspicious about who would do this to their leader. In Matthew and John's accounts, Judas Iscariot is identified as the betrayer (**Matthew 26:25; John 13:26**).

Judas was at the Last Supper with Jesus and the disciples. The fact that it was possible for a betrayer to be so close to the inner circle, even to participate in the initiation of the New Covenant (even if he apparently did not finish the meal), should serve as fair warning to all that it is possible for the enemy to infiltrate the ranks of the faithful and even to "break bread" with them. Fred Craddock called this a "continuing warning" (**Luke, 257**).

Commentators agree that there is a deliberate interplay with the dual mention of the Son of man being betrayed by a man. That the betrayal was "determined" meaning to appoint, decree, or ordain (used only eight times; e.g., **Acts 10:42; Romans 1:4; Hebrews 4:7**). Liefeld believes the point is that even though the events were ordained, Judas is still responsible for his role: "Divine sovereignty is balanced by human responsibility; so Jesus pronounces a 'woe' on the betrayer" (**Matthew, Mark, Luke, 1027**). Satan used Judas to fulfill God's plans. Yet, Judas' sin was not excused. And instead of repenting, he committed suicide (**Matthew 27:3–5**).

QUESTION 2

What was the reaction of the disciples upon hearing the news of Jesus' revelation of His betrayal?

They inquired among themselves who would do such a thing.

LIGHT ON THE WORD

Who's The Greatest?

Jesus had just told His disciples about His impending death, when a dispute arose among them over who was the greatest (**Luke 22:24**). They were only concerned about themselves. It is very easy to lose focus and start to think about ourselves as better than others. The disciples were a group of strong-willed men who felt they were very important. This happens in today's churches, too.

III. CALLED TO SERVE (Luke 22:24–30)

Jesus told the disciples the one who serves is the greatest (**verse 26**). We can look to Jesus as the example. Even though He could rightly claim His Messiahship, He came into the world to minister to us. We need Him. He did not need us. Therefore, we are to bow down and serve Him. By giving His life for us, He exemplified servanthood at its finest. We, too, should humble ourselves and serve others just as Jesus did for us. Then one day, we will all sit together in God's kingdom and celebrate at the wedding feast with the Lamb of God (**verse 30**).

Servant Leader (verses 24–30)

24 And there was also a strife among them, which of them should be accounted the greatest. 25 And he said unto them, The kings of the Gentiles exercise lordship over them; and they that exercise authority upon them are called benefactors. 26 But ye shall not be so: but he that is greatest among you, let him be as the younger; and he that is chief, as he that doth serve. 27 For whether is greater, he that sitteth at meat, or he that serveth? is not he that sitteth at meat? but I am among you as he that serveth. 28 Ye are they which have continued with me in my temptations. 29 And I appoint unto you a kingdom, as my Father hath appointed unto me; 30 That ye may eat and drink at my table in my kingdom, and sit on thrones judging the twelve tribes of Israel.

The argument the disciples were having was about who would sit where, since ancient seating customs put the most honored and important guests the closest to the host. The example of Jesus' own life gives weight to His teaching on the subject—He started the meal by washing their feet, a task relegated only to servants (**John 13:4–16**); He has come to serve, not to be served (**Matthew 20:28**); and His whole purpose is to do His Father's will (**John 8:28**). In the kingdom of God, true greatness doesn't seek self-veneration but is content with a lower place. In God's kingdom, everything is upside down and inside out; thus the servant, not the king, is called the benefactor. It must have been humbling for them to have their shallow argument exposed, especially when Jesus Himself had just washed their feet (**John 13:12–17**). As Fred Craddock notes, "True exaltation is, therefore, God's gift to those who faithfully endure the hardships of Christ" (**Luke, 258**).

The symbolism of Passover could not have been more perfect for the timing of the Passion of Christ. Craddock captures the essence: "This is no unimportant detail, for the Jewish Passover not only serves as backdrop for the Christian Table of Remembrance but the celebration of liberation from slavery in Egypt provides directly and indirectly meanings for the Lord's Supper" (**Luke, 253**). In retrospect, believers today know that God planned far in advance the details of both events, including the intentional interweaving of symbolism. At the time, none of the actors on the ancient stages were fully aware of the meaning of the events occurring before their eyes. Every element of the Passover meal contained reminders of Egypt—just as the elements of the Exodus carried prototypes of Jesus' Passion.

The Lord's Supper, also known as Communion (see **1 Corinthians 10:16**) and Eucharist (**Luke 22:17**), is only one of two sacraments (some call them ordinances) that Jesus personally instituted. Just as humans are inherently sinful, we also are inherently forgetful; thus the need for Jesus' instructions to keep this memorial alive so we will always remember His sacrifice. Far above and beyond the actual remembrance of Jesus' death, however, simple fellowship is often called "breaking bread" to this day. In Craddock's words, "Because of this last supper, no meal among disciples is just a meal, because no loaf is just bread, no cup is just wine" (**Luke, 255**).

QUESTION 3

Jesus says that the greatest do what?

Serve.

BIBLE APPLICATION

AIM: That your students will understand how they can glorify God through service to others.

Serve For God's Glory

We all are called to be God's servants. In today's lesson, we examined how Jesus' sacrifice on our behalf was an act of service. There are many people who are leaders but not servants. They dictate to others what to do and demand complete obedience. God wants us to be servants. In our service, we show humility and love of others. Jesus is our example of a servant-leader. His ministry on earth consisted of teaching, preaching, and healings. Jesus also performed many miracles. And then, Jesus offered His body as a sacrifice for all humanity. He did not do these things for personal glory. Jesus wanted His Father to be glorified. Whatever we do and say should be done for the glory of God.

STUDENTS' RESPONSES

AIM: That your students will be encouraged to proactively seek opportunities to bless others.

Every day we see people in need at work, in the community, and in church. Yet, we either ignore them or tell someone else to help them. Some of us would rather not humble ourselves and reach out to help. To do something for others may cause us to come out of our comfort zone. Yet, Jesus gave up His throne in heaven and came to earth to save us. He went about teaching, preaching, and healing people without thought of Himself. Jesus is our example of a servant. What are you willing to do to make a difference in someone's life, the community, and the world? Today, you can start by looking around your church and paying attention to what needs to be done. Commit to doing one thing every week and see the difference your service makes at home, in the community, at church, and in the world.

PRAYER

Dear Father, we humble ourselves in Your awesome presence and ask that You would use us to be a blessing to someone in need.

Thank You for strategically placing us in areas of need, and we pray to promptly obey just as the Lord Jesus did in His earthly ministry. Help us to serve and not be served. In Jesus' name, we pray. Amen.

DIG A LITTLE DEEPER

The Lord's Supper was instituted during Jesus' last Passover celebration with His disciples. Jesus symbolically aligned the bread and wine with His soon to be broken body and shed blood. He promised to share in this celebration again in the kingdom of God. This New Covenant is an example of the highest sacrifice or service which is the giving of one's life for another. Paul teaches us that Jesus wants to share in this celebration to remember his sacrifice. The believer's participation in the Lord's Supper should propel sacrificial giving of themselves for the benefit of others. During the early church, the Lord's Supper was an opportunity to fellowship and build community. It was a symbol shared among all the new believers. Even today, believers across the world are united through the partaking of the Lord's Supper. While we remember Jesus' sacrifice, how often do we go forth and look for a way to serve others? Can we combine evangelism, outreach, and communion? Our lesson challenges us to move beyond the ceremonial exercise of just saying "Hosanna".

HOW TO SAY IT

Atonement.	uh-TONE-muhnt.
Eucharist.	yoo-kuh-rust.
Hallel.	hah-LAYL.

Passover.   PAS-o-ver.

Testament.   teh-stuh-muhnt.

Liefeld, Walter L. Matthew, Mark, Luke. The Exposi- tor's Bible Commentary, vol. 8. Edited by Frank E. Gaebelein. Grand Rapids, MI: Zondervan, 1984. 1025–1028.
Life Application Bible – New Revised Standard Version. Wheaton, IL: Tyndale House Publishers, 1989. 1803.
Merriam-Webster Online Dictionary. http://www. merriam-webster.com (accessed November 3, 2011).
New Testament Greek Lexicon. http://www.biblestu- dytools.com/lexicons/greek (accessed May 6 and October 29, 2011).
Old and New Testament Concordances, Lexicons, Dictionaries, Commentaries, Images, and Bible Ver- sions. Blue Letter Bible.org. http://www.blueletter- bible.org/ (accessed April 20, 2011).
Smith, William. Smith's Bible Dictionary. http://www. biblestudytools.com/dictionaries/smiths-bible- dictionary.html (accessed May 5, 2011).

DAILY HOME BIBLE READINGS

MONDAY
Keeping the Passover to the Lord
(Deuteronomy 16:1–8)

TUESDAY
What Does This Observance Mean?
(Exodus 12:21–27)

WEDNESDAY
Preparations for the Last Supper
(Luke 22:7–13)

THURSDAY
Partaking of the Lord's Table
(1 Corinthians 10:14–22)

FRIDAY
Showing Contempt for the Church
(1 Corinthians 11:17–22)

SATURDAY
Examine Yourselves
(1 Corinthians 11:23–32)

SUNDAY
The Last Supper
(Luke 22:14–30)

COMMENTS / NOTES:

PREPARE FOR NEXT SUNDAY

Read **Luke 24:13–21, 28–35**, and study "The Lord Has Risen Indeed!"

Sources:
Barclay, William. The Gospel of Luke. The New Daily Study Bible. Louisville, KY: Westminster John Knox Press, 2001. 311–318.
Bock, Darrell L. Luke. IVP New Testament Commen- tary Series. Downers Grove, IL: InterVarsity Press, 1994. 345–355.
Craddock, Fred B. Luke. Interpretation: A Bible Com- mentary for Teaching and Preaching. Louisville, KY: Westminster John Knox Press, 1990. 252–260.
Gill, John. John Gill's Exposition of the Bible. http://www.biblestudytools.com/commentaries/gills-exposition-of-the-bible/Luke-22.html(accessed May 6, 2011).

THE LORD HAS RISEN INDEED! (EASTER)

BIBLE BASIS: Luke 24:13–21, 28–35

BIBLE TRUTH: The Resurrection of Jesus Christ is our hope.

MEMORY VERSE: "And their eyes were opened, and they knew him; and he vanished out of their sight" (Luke 24:31, KJV).

LESSON AIM: By the end of the lesson, we will: UNDERSTAND the power of a relationship with the risen Christ; REFLECT on the resurrection of our Savior; and DEVELOP a desire to share the message of the Gospel.

BACKGROUND SCRIPTURES: Luke 24:1–35, KJV — Read and incorporate the insights gained from the Background Scriptures into your study of the lesson.

TEACHER PREPARATION

MATERIALS NEEDED: Bibles, (several different versions), Quarterly Commentary/Teacher Manual, Adult Quarterly, teaching resources such as charts, worksheets/handouts, paper, pens, and pencils.

OTHER MATERIALS NEEDED / TEACHER'S NOTES:

_____

_____

LESSON OVERVIEW

LIFE NEED FOR TODAY'S LESSON

To understand the power of a relationship with the risen Christ.

BIBLE LEARNING

Jesus opened the eyes of two followers He encountered on the road to Emmaus.

BIBLE APPLICATION

To appreciate that Jesus is still opening eyes to the power of His Resurrection today.

STUDENTS' RESPONSES

Students will reflect on the Resurrection of our Savior and share the Gospel with others.

LESSON SCRIPTURE

LUKE 24:13–21, 28–35, KJV

13. And, behold, two of them went that same day to a village called Emmaus, which was from Jerusalem about threescore furlongs.

14. And they talked together of all these things which had happened.

15. And it came to pass, that, while they communed together and reasoned, Jesus himself drew near, and went with them.

16. But their eyes were holden that they should not know him.

47

17. And he said unto them, What manner of communications are these that ye have one to another, as ye walk, and are sad?

18. And the one of them, whose name was Cleopas, answering said unto him, Art thou only a stranger in Jerusalem, and hast not known the things which are come to pass there in these days?

19. And he said unto them, What things? And they said unto him, Concerning Jesus of Nazareth, which was a prophet mighty in deed and word before God and all the people:

20. And how the chief priests and our rulers delivered him to be condemned to death, and have crucified him.

21. But we trusted that it had been he which should have redeemed Israel: and beside all this, to day is the third day since these things were done.

24:28. And they drew nigh unto the village, whither they went: and he made as though he would have gone further.

29. But they constrained him, saying, Abide with us: for it is toward evening, and the day is far spent. And he went in to tarry with them.

30. And it came to pass, as he sat at meat with them, he took bread, and blessed it, and brake, and gave to them.

31. And their eyes were opened, and they knew him; and he vanished out of their sight.

32. And they said one to another, Did not our heart burn within us, while he talked with us by the way, and while he opened to us the scriptures?

33. And they rose up the same hour, and returned to Jerusalem, and found the eleven gathered together, and them that were with them,

34. Saying, The Lord is risen indeed, and hath appeared to Simon.

35. And they told what things were done in the way, and how he was known of them in breaking of bread.

BIBLICAL DEFINITIONS

A. Opened (Luke 24:31) *dianoigo* (Gk.)—Opened the mind or soul of someone; facilitated understanding.

B. Burn (v. 32) *kaio* (Gk.)—To set on fire, light.

LIGHT ON THE WORD

The disciples hoped that Jesus would be their Redeemer. The Israelites believed God would send the Messiah, who would overthrow the Roman government and free them from bondage. But now that He was dead, it seemed like all their hope was gone. They did not know what to believe about the reports of the empty tomb. He did say that on the third day He would be resurrected. The two men did not realize Jesus was the Redeemer of the world, who opened the way for all to be redeemed from the bondage of sin and death.

TEACHING THE BIBLE LESSON

LIFE NEED FOR TODAY'S LESSON

AIM: That your students will know that Jesus offers hope in the midst of despair.

INTRODUCTION

He Arose

After the betrayal of Jesus by Judas for 30 pieces of silver, He was arrested and taken to trial. It was an illegal trial, and He was condemned to die on the Cross. Before they nailed His hands and feet to the Cross, Jesus was beaten, mocked, and pierced by a crown of thorns. Upon His death, the disciples went into hiding in Jerusalem, afraid that they, too, would be crucified as followers of Christ.

Mary Magdalene, Joanna, Mary the mother of James, and other women visited the tomb where they laid Jesus' body and found it empty (**Luke 24:1–11**). Peter did not believe the women, so he went to investigate the matter. He found the tomb empty and the burial clothes of Jesus folded nicely. The resurrected Jesus appeared to Mary Magdalene in the garden (**Mark 16:9**). He also appeared to other women (**Matthew 28:9–10**). These accounts of Jesus' resurrection appearances, as well as others, confirm that He kept His promise. He had predicted three times that He would suffer, die on the Cross, and be resurrected. In spite of all the evidence, some of His disciples still were hopeless and despondent.

BIBLE LEARNING

AIM: That your students will celebrate that Jesus has risen.

I. ON THE ROAD TO REVELATION (Luke 24:13–21)

After Jesus' death, all hope seemed lost for many of His followers. They thought Jesus would become their earthly king and overthrow the government, thus providing peace for the people. When this did not happen and Jesus was crucified, they did not know where or to whom to turn for help. Two men, one named Cleopas, decided to head back to Emmaus. We do not know what they planned on doing when they arrived in Emmaus; we just know they were saddened by Jesus' death. However, their seven-mile journey was about to be interrupted by an unexpected traveler.

Hopelessness and Despair (verses 13–21)

13 And, behold, two of them went that same day to a village called Emmaus, which was from Jerusalem about three-score furlongs. 14 And they talked together of all these things which had happened. 15 And it came to pass, that, while they communed together and reasoned, Jesus himself drew near, and went with them. 16 But their eyes were holden that they should not know him. 17 And he said unto them, What manner of communications are these that ye have one to another, as ye walk, and are sad? 18 And the one of them, whose name was Cleopas, answering said unto him, Art thou only a stranger in Jerusalem, and hast not known the things which are come to pass there in these days? 19 And he said unto them, What things? And they said unto him, Concerning Jesus of Nazareth, which was a prophet mighty in deed and word before God and all the people: 20 And how the chief priests and our rulers delivered him to be condemned to death, and have crucified him. 21 But we trusted that it had been he which should have redeemed Israel: and beside all this, to day is the third day since these things were done.

After the women's report and Peter's confirmation, two of the disciples decided to go to the village of Emmaus, which was about 7 miles or 11 kilometers ("about threescore furlongs") from Jerusalem. The precise location of Emmaus is uncertain because there are two possible sites that we know of today. The disciples' motive for going there is not known. They may have been residents of Emmaus and prevented by the Sabbath and the surrounding events from getting back to their village. Their journey took place on the first day of the week. The phrase "that same day" indicates that this event took place on the day the women went to the tomb. Chronologically, it came after the women's visit to the tomb, and it probably came after Peter and John's visit to the tomb, as is made clear later in the text.

The two disciples discussed the report of the women and that of Peter. The subject of their discussions was not only on the empty tomb but also more on the succession of events since

49

the betrayal of Jesus. They should have rejoiced because the One they were discussing had joined them and was alive. However, they were kept from recognizing Him. The Greek wording used in **verse 16** says that their eyes were "holden" meaning "restrained" from recognizing Him. This prevention is either coming from their unbelief due to their sorrow—because **Mark 16:10** mentions that the disciples were mourning and weeping— or it may be that God intentionally prevented them from recognizing Him.

Jesus' question was a probing inquiry. He knew what they were discussing. Jesus knew the thoughts of His disciples and His audience before these people even spoke (see, for example, **Matthew 12:25; Mark 12:14–15; Luke 9:47**). Jesus knew their subject of discussion but more than that, He knew their state of mind. In reaction to Jesus' question, they expressed their discouragement and sorrow. Their hearts were not at peace. Jesus knew their doubts, and He wanted to provide them with healing.

In reply to Jesus' inquiry, one of these disciples named Cleopas was concerned. Much is not known about this disciple apart from the mention of his name. His reply to Jesus tells us the extent to which the public knew about the events concerning Jesus' trial and death. "These days" do not include this particular day, Sunday. They may be referring to the day of Jesus' triumphal entry in Jerusalem up to His burial on Friday.

The event of the missing body in the tomb was fresh news not yet known to the public. Jesus asked for clarification about the things that happened. The disciples clarified to Him their concept of things that occurred: they spoke of things that happened "Concerning Jesus of Nazareth, which was a prophet" (**verse 19**). They then gave a powerful testimony of Jesus' words and deeds.

Their hope was based on Jesus delivering Israel from Roman occupation. They misunderstood the Messianic role of Jesus. They might have been influenced by the prevailing ideas about Christ among the Jews.

"The third day" was a date Jesus gave to His disciples as the day of His Resurrection from the dead. Predictions have meanings when they are kept and considered faithfully. Daniel could recognize, for example, that the 70 years of the Israelites' captivity was over, and he decided to intercede for the people in exile (**Daniel 9:1–3**). Here, it is possible that the disciples' sorrow has made them forget even the predictions of the Resurrection on the third day, because the angels reminded the women of what Jesus had told His followers (**Luke 24:6**). Even with this reminder, the two disciples' situation did not allow a proper attitude of expectation like Daniel possessed. The third day was a promised day that they should have eagerly awaited, but sorrow and distress made them forget its promise.

SEARCH THE SCRIPTURES

QUESTION 1

How far was Emmaus from Jerusalem?

Three score furlongs or seven miles.

LIGHT ON THE WORD

Slow of Heart to Believe

Because His suffering, death, and Resurrection are revealed in Scripture, and they should have known the truth, Jesus scolded the two men for their unbelief (**verses 25–26**). He then interpreted the Old Testament and explained to them the prophecies that referred to Him (**verse 27**). The suffering, death, and Resurrection of Jesus brought to fulfillment the prophecies contained in the law, prophets, and writings.

II. A CONVERSATION WORTH CONTINUING (Luke 24:28–35)

As the two men and Jesus approached Emmaus, Jesus continued walking (**verse 28**). He was not going to continue with the two men unless invited. Jesus waits for us to invite Him in. They urged Him to stay with them since it was late (**verse 29**). It is unknown whether it was their home, a friend's house, or a temporary place of rest. No matter, Jesus still went in to stay with them. Since it was so enlightening, the two men wanted to continue the conversation they were having.

Hope Restored (verses 28–35)
28 And they drew nigh unto the village, whither they went: and he made as though he would have gone further. 29 But they constrained him, saying, Abide with us: for it is toward evening, and the day is far spent. And he went in to tarry with them. 30 And it came to pass, as he sat at meat with them, he took bread, and blessed it, and brake, and gave to them. 31 And their eyes were opened, and they knew him; and he vanished out of their sight. 32 And they said one to another, Did not our heart burn within us, while he talked with us by the way, and while he opened to us the scriptures? 33 And they rose up the same hour, and returned to Jerusalem, and found the eleven gathered together, and them that were with them, 34 Saying, The Lord is risen indeed, and hath appeared to Simon. 35 And they told what things were done in the way, and how he was known of them in breaking of bread.

When Jesus and the disciples were traveling along the road to Emmaus, He acts as though He will continue His journey. Because it was getting late, they urged Him to stay the night with them. Hospitality is part of Jewish culture. The writer of Hebrews urges his readers to welcome strangers (**Hebrews 13:2**). We should be encouraged to practice hospitality with caution and by the discernment the Spirit grants to believers.

The hospitality these two disciples offered to Jesus strongly suggests that they are from Emmaus. If that were not the case, it would have been difficult for them to host someone else, because they would have been guests themselves. One argument that favors this view is that they almost "constrained" Jesus to stay with them (**verse 29**). The powerful way Jesus explained the Scripture to them had certainly played a role in their invitation also. They might have been willing to hear more and the sudden parting of their companion would have deprived them.

"And it came to pass, as he sat at meat with them, he took bread, and blessed it, and brake, and gave to them" (**verse 30**). The meal Jesus shared with the two men was the Lord's Supper. It is the presence of Christ, at the table opened to a stranger, which transforms an ordinary meal into the Eucharist. Based on the language, we can see the similarities from previous meals (**Luke 22:19**). It is in the midst of Jesus taking bread, blessing and breaking it, and sharing with the men, that their eyes opened. However, they did not enjoy His presence for long because He disappeared from their sight (**verse 31**). This disappearance does not make Jesus' resurrected body immaterial. Had it been so, He could not have eaten with them. In addition, we know that Philip was taken away after baptizing the Ethiopian eunuch (**Acts 8:39**). Though some suggest it was not a supernatural occurrence, the testimony of Jesus' different appearances and sudden disappearances proves that it was supernatural and may be a characteristic of the resurrected body. Jesus' teachings caused their "hearts to burn within" them (**verse 32**). **Jeremiah 23:29a** (NIV) states, "Is not my word like fire....?" God's Word is so powerful that it can illuminate even the darkest place of the soul. These two men had experienced sadness and hopelessness, until the Word and sacrament were shared with them. Jesus restored their hope. The two disciples returned to Jerusalem that night and witnessed to the 11 apostles and the other disciples, both men and women (**verse 33**).

Just as the two disciples entered the place where the apostles and others had gathered, the apostles declared, "The Lord is risen indeed, and hath appeared to Simon" (**verse 34**). In spite of His denial, Jesus did appear to Simon Peter first as a means of communicating His love and grace toward Him. Paul mentions in **1 Corinthians 15:5** that Jesus appeared to Cephas, Peter's Greek surname. The two disciples who had just arrived witnessed to others about their encounter with Jesus on the road to Emmaus (**verse 35**). Their witness along with the others offered hope and encouragement to the believers.

QUESTION 2

What happened when Jesus sat with the two disciples for a meal?

Jesus blessed the food, broke the bread, they recognized Jesus, and He vanishes from their sight.

BIBLE APPLICATION

AIM: That your students take comfort in knowing that our God reigns.

Share the Good News

Whatever their reason for coming back to Emmaus, it became secondary in comparison to the news of their encounter with Jesus. The two men in our Scripture lesson went from being hopeless to hopeful. Then, they went back to Jerusalem to share the exciting news of the Resurrection with the other disciples. In overcoming death, Jesus truly is the Lord of lords, the King of kings.

STUDENTS' RESPONSES

AIM: That your students will boldly share the Gospel of Jesus Christ to offer hope to a dying world.

We can often get entangled in our own sense of grief and despair. In today's lesson, we will learn that Jesus offers hope to us no matter the circumstances we face. This week, we may encounter people who are experiencing difficulties in their families, financial problems, sickness, the loss of a loved one, etc. We can show compassion toward others by listening to them and sharing the message of the Gospel. Like the disciples on the road to Emmaus, we too have a message of hope for a hurting world. Let's share the message wherever we go.

PRAYER

Lord, we celebrate Your resurrection today and every day. Thank You for giving us victory over sin, and death, for freedom, and by faith reconciling us back to the Father. Forgive us for times You are revealing Yourself to us, by the Holy Spirit and the Word, and we are slow of heart to believe. Change our hearts, Lord, so that we are able to believe You and not doubt. We pray our love and faith will draw others unto You. In Jesus' name, we pray. Amen.

DIG A LITTLE DEEPER

At what point will you believe that Jesus has risen? What record would you believe? In our lesson today, it is apparent these two disciples were a part of the close group of followers of Jesus. They were hiding with Jesus' disciples during the passion of Christ. I can imagine by now the rumors were circulating that the disciples had taken the body, Peter confirmed Jesus' body wasn't in the tomb, and Mary Magdalene claimed she had seen Jesus. These disciples decided it was probably best to go home. While they were on the way home, Jesus started walking and talking with them expounding the Scriptures and it wasn't until Jesus broke bread and blessed it that their eyes were open that Jesus was alive. Why couldn't they believe the prophecies recorded in the scrolls? Didn't Jesus fulfill all of them? Why wouldn't they believe Mary's report of seeing and speaking with Jesus? Why would it take an actual visit by Jesus for them to believe? We must believe God's Word and the testimonies of witnesses of Jesus' miracles. These two sources serve as the primary record of God's truth that will bring hope. We cannot allow the limitations of our minds which bring doubt and discrimination to prevent us from our responsibility to share the good news of Jesus with the world.

HOW TO SAY IT:

Cleopas.	KLEE–o-pas.
Emmaus.	eh-MAY-uhs.
Jerusalem.	jeh-ROO-suh-lehm.

PREPARE FOR NEXT SUNDAY

Read—**Luke 24:36-53**, and study "The Lord Appears."

Sources:

Barnes, Albert. Notes on the New Testament: Luke and John. Grand Rapids, MI: Baker Book House, 1965.

Biblical Words Pronunciation Guide. http://netminis-tries.org/Bbasics/bwords.htm (accessed November 3, 2011).

Black, Mark C. The College Press NIV Commentary: Luke. Joplin, MO: College Press Publishing, 1996.

Butler, Paul T. Bible Study Textbook Series: Gospel of Luke. Joplin, MO: College Press Publishing, 1981.

Craddock, Fred B. Interpretation: A Bible Commentary for Teaching and Preaching (Luke). Louisville, KY: John Knox Press, 1990. 279-288.

Gill, John. John Gill's Exposition of the Bible. http:// www.biblestudytools.com/commentaries/gills-   exposition-of-the-bible/Luke-24.html (accessed May 6, 2011).

Life Application Bible – New Revised Standard Version. Wheaton, IL: Tyndale House Publishers, 1989. 1811-1812.

Morris, Leon. Tyndale New Testament Commentaries: Luke. Grand Rapids, MI: Wm. B. Eerdmans, 1986.

New Testament Greek Lexicon. http://www.biblestu- dytools.com/lexicons/greek (accessed May 9 and October 29, 2011).

Smith, William. Smith's Bible Dictionary. http://www. biblestudytools.com/dictionaries/smiths-bible- dictionary.html (accessed May 5, 2011).

DAILY HOME BIBLE READINGS

MONDAY
The Trial before Pilate
(Luke 23:13–25)

TUESDAY
The Crucifixion of Jesus
(Luke 23:32–38)

WEDNESDAY
The Death of Jesus
(Luke 23:44–49)

THURSDAY
The Burial of Jesus
(Luke 23:50–56)

FRIDAY
The Messiah's Suffering
(Isaiah 53:3–9)

SATURDAY
Discovery of the Empty Tomb
(Luke 24:1–12)

SUNDAY
The Lord Has Risen Indeed!
(Luke 24:13–21, 28–35)

COMMENTS / NOTES:

_____
_____
_____
_____
_____
_____
_____
_____
_____
_____
_____
_____
_____

THE LORD APPEARS

BIBLE BASIS: Luke 24:36–53

BIBLE TRUTH: Jesus keeps His promises.

MEMORY VERSE: "And he said unto them, These are the words which I spake unto you, while I was yet with you, that all things must be fulfilled, which were written in the law of Moses, and in the prophets, and in the psalms, concerning me" (Luke 24:44, KJV).

LESSON AIM: By the end of the lesson, we will: DESCRIBE the assurance of the power of the Holy Spirit; REFLECT on the power of God displayed in Scripture; and DECIDE to seek the fulfillment of all that Jesus has promised us.

BACKGROUND SCRIPTURES: Luke 24:36-53, KJV — Read and incorporate the insights gained from the Background Scriptures into your study of the lesson.

TEACHER PREPARATION

MATERIALS NEEDED: Bibles, (several different versions), Quarterly Commentary/Teacher Manual, Adult Quarterly, teaching resources such as charts, worksheets/handouts, paper, pens, and pencils.

OTHER MATERIALS NEEDED / TEACHER'S NOTES:

_____

_____

LESSON OVERVIEW

LIFE NEED FOR TODAY'S LESSON

To observe God's power displayed in Scripture.

BIBLE LEARNING

Jesus kept His Word and fulfilled the words of prophecy about Him.

BIBLE APPLICATION

To understand God's power displayed in Scripture.

STUDENTS' RESPONSES

Students will discern the fulfillment of the life Jesus promised.

LESSON SCRIPTURE

LUKE 24:36–53, KJV

36. And as they thus spake, Jesus himself stood in the midst of them, and saith unto them, Peace be unto you.

37. But they were terrified and affrighted, and supposed that they had seen a spirit.

38. And he said unto them, Why are ye troubled? and why do thoughts arise in your hearts?

39. Behold my hands and my feet, that it is I myself: handle me, and see; for a spirit hath not flesh and bones, as ye see me have.

54

40. And when he had thus spoken, he shewed them his hands and his feet.

41. And while they yet believed not for joy, and wondered, he said unto them, Have ye here any meat?

42. And they gave him a piece of a broiled fish, and of an honeycomb.

43. And he took it, and did eat before them.

44. And he said unto them, These are the words which I spake unto you, while I was yet with you, that all things must be fulfilled, which were written in the law of Moses, and in the prophets, and in the psalms, concerning me.

45. Then opened he their understanding, that they might understand the scriptures,

46. And said unto them, Thus it is written, and thus it behooved Christ to suffer, and to rise from the dead the third day:

47. And that repentance and remission of sins should be preached in his name among all nations, beginning at Jerusalem.

48. And ye are witnesses of these things.

49. And, behold, I send the promise of my Father upon you: but tarry ye in the city of Jerusalem, until ye be endued with power from on high.

50. And he led them out as far as to Bethany, and he lifted up his hands, and blessed them.

51. And it came to pass, while he blessed them, he was parted from them, and carried up into heaven.

52. And they worshipped him, and returned to Jerusalem with great joy:

53. And were continually in the temple, praising and blessing God. Amen.

BIBLICAL DEFINITIONS

A. Fulfilled (Luke 24:44) *pleroo* (Gk.)—Made complete, rendered perfect.
B. Promise (v. 49) *epaggelia* (Gk.)—An announcement.

LIGHT ON THE WORD

On the third day after the death of Christ, two disciples encountered the resurrected Jesus on their way to Emmaus (Luke 24:13– 21, 28–35). Because they were so grief stricken, they were unaware it was Jesus. He opened the Scriptures to them and revealed the Old Testament prophecies that spoke of the Messiah. After such sadness and despondency over the death of their leader, His words restored their hope. They invited Him to stay with them since it was so late when they arrived in Emmaus. They shared the Lord's Supper. Immediately, they recognized who Jesus was, and He disappeared. Their hearts burned within them as Jesus shared the Word and their faith became revitalized. They immediately returned to Jerusalem to witness to the other disciples about their encounter with the resurrected Savior. Today's text tells us of Jesus' appearance to the disciples and His ascension.

TEACHING THE BIBLE LESSON

LIFE NEED FOR TODAY'S LESSON

AIM: That your students will know that Jesus is the fulfillment of God's promises.

INTRODUCTION

Jerusalem the Epicenter of Jewish History

Jerusalem was the central religious and political area for Israel. After David transfers the Ark of the Covenant to Jerusalem (2 Samuel 6:12-15), Jerusalem becomes the central place that leaders, judges, prophets, and people are affiliated with in some way. This is also true of the New Testament. In the beginning of the Book of Luke, he opens with a scene from the

Temple where Zechariah is worshiping and is told by an angel of the Lord that John the Baptist would be born (**1:8–17**). Immediately following that announcement, the birth of Jesus is foretold (**1:26–38**). Throughout the Book of Luke, we are given hints that Jerusalem is where all the most important events will occur. So it is no surprise that Jesus predicted that His suffering on the Cross, death, and Resurrection would occur in Jerusalem. We end the book with Jesus' followers worshiping in the Temple in Jerusalem (**24:52–53**).

BIBLE LEARNING

AIM: That your students will reflect on the convincing proofs of Jesus' Resurrection.

I. RENEWED HOPE (Luke 24:36–43)

It's very late at night when Cleopas and the other disciple arrive back in Jerusalem. Their journey from Emmaus was seven miles, and lest we forget, it is the same day that Jesus was resurrected from the dead. The 11 apostles and others assembled surely had to be surprised to see them again, especially at such a late hour. Cleopas and the other disciple felt the need to share the renewed hope they had experienced after encountering Jesus on the road to Emmaus.

Jesus' Private Appearance to the Disciples (Luke 24:36–43)

36 And as they thus spake, Jesus himself stood in the midst of them, and saith unto them, Peace be unto you. 37 But they were terrified and affrighted, and supposed that they had seen a spirit. 38 And he said unto them, Why are ye troubled? and why do thoughts arise in your hearts? 39 Behold my hands and my feet, that it is I myself: handle me, and see; for a spirit hath not flesh and bones, as ye see me have. 40 And when he had thus spoken, he shewed them his hands and his feet. 41 And while they yet believed not for joy, and wondered, he said unto them, Have ye here any meat? 42 And they gave him a piece of a broiled fish, and of an honeycomb. 43 And he took it, and did eat before them.

Gathered at Jerusalem in the Upper Room that will be their place of meeting for the coming days (**John 20:19; Acts 1:13; 2:1**), the disciples were discussing Jesus' appearance to Peter and the two disciples on the road to Emmaus. Then, Jesus appeared again to all of them with the exception of Thomas. This event occurred in the evening of the first day of Jesus' Resurrection. We learn from the Gospel of John that the disciples closed the door for fear of the Jews. Jesus standing before them with the door closed is not surprising. Even before His resurrection, He demonstrated His supernatural ability; for instance, He walked on water. So it is not strange that He could suddenly appear in their midst without opening a door or window.

Jesus greeted them in the traditional fashion in the Jews' community (**Luke 24:36**). "Peace be unto you" was a standard greeting that expressed hope for peace and prosperity to the recipient. They needed peace in these moments of confusion. Jesus was the One who could give them true peace (**John 14:27**). Not only does He give us peace, but He is in fact our peace. They were terrified and thought Jesus was a spirit (**Luke 24:37**). This is in spite of the reports of the two women, Simon Peter, and the two disciples who had just arrived from Emmaus. They still did not believe it was Jesus. More than likely, the apostles thought they were seeing the dead. How else could they explain Jesus' sudden appearance?

Jesus questioned why they were so frightened and filled with doubt that it was actually Him (**verse 38**). Did they forget that He foretold the events and His resurrection? After all the evidence they had that Jesus had arisen from the grave, they still doubted His promise of being resurrected on the third day. Jesus offered as evidence His nailed-pierced hands and feet for the apostles and others to see and touch (**verses 39–40**). Some may not have believed it was Jesus unless they could touch His body. However, as Christians, we should "walk by faith, not by sight" (**2 Corinthians 5:7**).

While the disciples were overjoyed at being able to see the resurrected Jesus, some still had doubts about the reality of what they were experiencing (**Luke 24:41**). Once again, to prove to the believers gathered that it really was Jesus in the flesh, He ate some fish and honeycomb (**verses 42–43**). This demonstrated He had a physical body that could consume food.

SEARCH THE SCRIPTURES
QUESTION 1

What did Jesus say when He first appeared to His disciples?

Peace be unto you.

LIGHT ON THE WORD
Convinced of the Resurrection

Jesus gives the disciples many convincing proofs of the resurrection of Christ in order to believe. Jesus appears to them many times and in various circumstances and gives them sufficient proof through three important senses of human beings: seeing, hearing, and touching. When they are convinced, He then instructs them on what to do next before His departure to His Father. It is clear from Acts that the last part of this week's Scripture text refers to the 40th day after Jesus' Resurrection.

II. A NEW AGENDA (Luke 24:44–49)

Jesus highlights a certain difference between His former relations with them and this new phase. "While I was yet with you" refers to His ministry before His death. In addition to His teaching and miracles, He shared all the peculiarities of

human life. He suffered hunger, thirst, tiredness, and pain. He expressed emotions, weeping when Lazarus died. In view of this, He is no longer present with His disciples in the same manner, though He is with them physically at this moment. He is no longer constrained by the laws of nature, and He has a different agenda now.

Jesus' Public Appearance in Jerusalem (verses 44–49)

44 And he said unto them, These are the words which I spake unto you, while I was yet with you, that all things must be fulfilled, which were written in the law of Moses, and in the prophets, and in the psalms, concerning me. 45 Then opened he their understanding, that they might understand the scriptures, 46 And said unto them, Thus it is written, and thus it behooved Christ to suffer, and to rise from the dead the third day: 47 And that repentance and remission of sins should be preached in his name among all nations, beginning at Jerusalem. 48 And ye are witnesses of these things. 49 And, behold, I send the promise of my Father upon you: but tarry ye in the city of Jerusalem, until ye be endued with power from on high.

Jesus had to fulfill all the Old Testament prophecies concerning the Messiah (**Genesis 3:15; 22:13; Isaiah 53; Psalm 16:10; 22**). He opened up the minds of His disciples by the power of the Holy Spirit, so they could understand the Scriptures. Jesus then reminded them that He had previously predicted His suffering, death, and Resurrection on the third day (**Matthew 16:21; 17:22–23; 20:18–19**). There is continuity from the Old Testament through the New Testament. God is faithful and keeps His promises. The apostles and disciples were witnesses to all He did. The words that He spoke were destined to be fulfilled, even before the beginning of all creation.

57

The Great Commission given in **Matthew 28:18-20** is repeated in **Luke 24:47-48**. They were told that "repentance and remission (forgiveness) of sins should be preached in his [Jesus'] name;" the message should be proclaimed "among all nations, beginning in Jerusalem" (**verse 47**). Our response to Jesus' sacrifice should be repentance of sins. When we repent, we will be forgiven. This is the core message of the Gospel. God's plan from the very beginning has been to extend His love and mercy toward all people, Jew or Gentile. However, the Jews had to have the first opportunity to hear the Gospel. In Jerusalem, the people involved in Christ's crucifixion needed to hear the Gospel message of repentance and forgiveness. This was accomplished at Pentecost (**Acts 2**). Then, the message was to be shared "in all Judaea, and in Samaria, and unto the uttermost part of the earth," which they accordingly did (**Acts 1:8**; see also **2:30-32; 10:39-41; 20:21**).

Jesus knew that His followers were not ready to preach the Gospel to all people and nations. He said, "I send the promise of my Father upon you: but tarry ye in the city of Jerusalem, until ye be endued with power from on high" (**Luke 24:49**). The promise was to receive power from God through the Holy Spirit. They had to wait until God decided they were ready to receive this power. God had them wait 50 days (from Easter to Pentecost). They used the time to worship and pray. The promise was fulfilled (**Acts 2:4**).

QUESTION 2

What did Jesus remind His followers?

That all things must be fulfilled, which were written in the Law of Moses, and in the prophets, and in the psalms, concerning Him.

LIGHT ON THE WORD

Who's The Greatest?

When Jesus had finished instructing them, He led them to Bethany. This scene occurred on the 40th day after His Resurrection. In this passage, it is difficult to differentiate between the event that happened the first day and what happened the 40th day. However, it is probable that Jesus' eating to convince them (**verse 43**) happened the first day, and verse 44 could be the beginning of the narrative of the 40th day's events. Regardless, in the last earthly scene of Jesus with the disciples, He lifted up His hands and blessed them. He prayed for them, their safety in an evil world, their unity for a convincing testimony, and He blessed them to have a fruitful ministry (**John 17**).

III. PROMISE FULFILLED (Luke 24:50-53)

Before the Resurrection, they referred to Jesus most often as Teacher or Master. After His appearance to Peter, they called Him by the title "Lord" (**verse 34**). And now they are filled with joy, ready to worship Him. They knew without a doubt that they were with the Lord of lords, the Son of God incarnate. He deserved their worship, and they will dedicate their lives to His service, even to the point of death. However, as He just recommended to them, they went back to Jerusalem to wait for the promise of the Father, the Holy Spirit. The fulfillment of the promise will be the green light for the start of their ministries.

Jesus' Ascension (verses 50-53)

50 And he led them out as far as to Bethany, and he lifted up his hands, and blessed them. 51 And it came to pass, while he blessed them, he was parted from them, and carried up into heaven. 52 And they worshipped him, and returned to Jerusalem with great joy: 53 And were continually in the temple, praising and blessing God. Amen.

Jesus led the apostles and disciples to a village on the Mount of Olives called Bethany. This Bethany is not the hometown of Jesus' friends: Mary, Martha, and Lazarus. This village was a mile away from Jerusalem and began at the Mount of Olives where Bethpage ended. It was here that Jesus chose to ascend into heaven.

Jesus "lifted up His hands and blessed them" (**Luke 24:50, NKJV**). The blessing is a priestly act in which Jesus places His followers in the care and favor of God. They would need to learn how to completely depend on God for all things. Most importantly, they needed God's Spirit to help them to understand the Word so as they prepare to go places and preach, lives may be transformed. We all need to remember God will provide and take care of us.

While He was blessing them, Jesus started to ascend into heaven (**verse 51**). They watched Him until He could no longer be seen. Jesus returned to heaven to be with His Father, who welcomed Him. The apostles and disciples were not sad at His departure because He had promised to send the Holy Spirit to be their guide and comforter. Moreover, they knew one day they would be reunited with Jesus. They began to worship Jesus because He is the Messiah, Savior, Resurrected One, Deliverer, Healer, and so much more.

The followers returned to Jerusalem and went to the Temple rejoicing for all they had experienced and what was yet to come (**verses 52–53**). They had expectations that the Holy Spirit would come just as Jesus promised. Jesus had given them hope for the future. They stayed in the Temple continually offering praise, prayers, and thanksgiving to God. We, too, should continually worship God and offer praise to His name for being our Savior and Lord.

QUESTION 3

Where did Jesus go after leading His followers to Bethany?

He was carried to heaven.

BIBLE APPLICATION

AIM: That your students will praise God for keeping His promises through Jesus Christ.

Serve For God's Glory

Promises made seem often hard to keep. In today's lesson, we saw how Jesus kept His promises and fulfilled all Old Testament prophecies. We learn to trust people based upon their words. Jesus proved He is trustworthy because He has fulfilled every promise made. He wants us to trust Him unconditionally and seek to live out His promises. In today's society, it can be difficult living out the promises of God. What hindrances do you face in seeking to fulfill God's promises? How can you overcome the stumbling blocks?

STUDENTS' RESPONSES

AIM: That your students will reflect on God's promises fulfilled in their lives.

Jesus appeared to the disciples to prove that He had been resurrected and to give reassurance to them. Sometimes we need evidence before we believe promises made by others. Jesus' life, death, and Resurrection fulfilled all the prophecies of the Old Testament about the Messiah. He is trustworthy. What promises has God made to you through His Word? There is no need to delay in seeking the fulfillment of God's promises for your life. This week, write down the promises and corresponding Scriptures. Pray and ask God for guidance in the steps to take. Step out by faith and take action. "Every word of God proves true."

PRAYER

Dear Father, we humble ourselves in Your awesome presence and ask that You would use us to be a blessing to someone in need. Thank You for strategically placing us in areas of need, and we pray to promptly obey just as the Lord

Jesus did in His earthly ministry. Help us to serve and not be served. In Jesus' name, we pray. Amen.

DIG A LITTLE DEEPER

As we continue in the Lukan post-resurrection appearances, we see Jesus make His final earthly appearance to His disciples before ascending back to heaven. During this visit, He reaffirmed His fulfillment of the Scriptures and challenged them to receive the Holy Ghost for their next phase of ministry. The disciple's reflection on the life Jesus fulfilled resulted in praises to God. Believers are to be encouraged that they are living on purpose with purpose. God has directed and constructed every phase of their lives. We are to look to Jesus as our example of how to trust God's plan. Jesus relied on the Word of God, prayer, and the leading of the Holy Ghost to know and fulfill His purpose on earth. In Jesus' communication with His disciples, He calms His disciples through His presence, assures them through the Word, and blesses them on His exit. We should reflect on our lives to see God's fulfillment of His promises to be able to deal with life's difficult seasons. We should be able to calm, assure, and bless others as we go forth and witness. If we live like Jesus, we too will one day reunite with our Father in heaven and leave a legacy that brings God glory.

HOW TO SAY IT

Bethany. BETH-uh-nee.

Benjamin.   BEN-juh-muhn.

DAILY HOME BIBLE READINGS

MONDAY
Appearances of the Risen Lord
(1 Corinthians 15:1–8)

TUESDAY
The Appearance to Mary Magdalene
(John 20:11–18)

WEDNESDAY
The Appearance to Thomas (
John 20:24–29)

THURSDAY
The Appearance to Seven Disciples
(John 21:1–8)

FRIDAY
Breakfast with the Disciples
(John 21:9–14)

SATURDAY
Simon Peter Called to Follow
(John 21:15–19)

SUNDAY
You Are Witnesses of These Things
(Luke 24:36–53)

PREPARE FOR NEXT SUNDAY

Read **Acts 2:1-13,** and study "The Holy Spirit Comes."

Sources:
Barnes, Albert. Notes on the New Testament: Luke and John. Grand Rapids, MI: Baker Book House, 1965.
Biblical Words Pronunciation Guide. http://netminis- tries.org/Bbasics/bwords.htm (accessed November 3, 2011).
Black, Mark C. The College Press NIV Commentary: Luke. Joplin, MO: College Press Publishing Com- pany, 1996.
Butler, Paul T. Bible Study Textbook Series: Gospel of Luke. Joplin, MO: College Press Publishing Com- pany, 1981.
Craddock, Fred B. Interpretation: A Bible Commen- tary for Teaching and Preaching (Luke). Louisville, KY: John Knox Press, 1990. 288-295.
Gill, John. John Gill's Exposition of the Bible. http:// www.biblestudytools.com/commen
Life Application Bible – New Revised Standard Version. Wheaton, IL: Tyndale House Publishers, 1989. 1812- 1813.
Morris, Leon. Tyndale New Testament Commentaries: Luke. Grand Rapids, MI: Wm. B. Eerdmans, 1986.
New Testament Greek Lexicon. http://www.biblestudy- tools.com/lexicons/greek (accessed May 10, 2011).
Smith, William. Smith's Bible Dictionary. http://www. biblestudytools.com/dictionaries/smiths-bible- dictionary.html (accessed May 7, 2011).

THE HOLY SPIRIT COMES

BIBLE BASIS: Acts 2:1–13

BIBLE TRUTH: The Holy Spirit provides life-transforming power.

MEMORY VERSE: "And they were all filled with the Holy Ghost, and began to speak with other tongues, as the Spirit gave them utterance" (Acts 2:4, KJV).

LESSON AIM: By the end of the lesson, we will: UNDERSTAND that God wants all people to know His love; APPRECIATE the value of living by faith; and COMMIT to a closer walk with God.

BACKGROUND SCRIPTURES: Acts 2:1–13, KJV — Read and incorporate the insights gained from the Background Scriptures into your study of the lesson.

TEACHER PREPARATION

MATERIALS NEEDED: Bibles, (several different versions), Quarterly Commentary/Teacher Manual, Adult Quarterly, teaching resources such as charts, worksheets/handouts, paper, pens, and pencils.

OTHER MATERIALS NEEDED / TEACHER'S NOTES:

_____

_____

LESSON OVERVIEW

LIFE NEED FOR TODAY'S LESSON

To remember the value of living by faith.

BIBLE LEARNING

The Holy Spirit is at work in a faithful heart.

BIBLE APPLICATION

To begin to understand how to live by faith through the power of the Holy Spirit.

STUDENTS' RESPONSES

Students will commit to developing a closer walk with God.

LESSON SCRIPTURE

ACTS 2:1–13, KJV

1. And when the day of Pentecost was fully come, they were all with one accord in one place.

2. And suddenly there came a sound from heaven as of a rushing mighty wind, and it filled all the house where they were sitting.

3. And there appeared unto them cloven tongues like as of fire, and it sat upon each of them.

4. And they were all filled with the Holy Ghost, and began to speak with other tongues, as the Spirit gave them utterance.

5. And there were dwelling at Jerusalem Jews, devout men, out of every nation under heaven.

6. Now when this was noised abroad, the multitude came together, and were confounded, because that every man heard them speak in his own language.

7. And they were all amazed and marvelled, saying one to another, Behold, are not all these which speak Galilaeans?

8. And how hear we every man in our own tongue, wherein we were born?

9. Parthians, and Medes, and Elamites, and the dwellers in Mesopotamia, and in Judaea, and Cappadocia, in Pontus, and Asia,

10. Phrygia, and Pamphylia, in Egypt, and in the parts of Libya about Cyrene, and strangers of Rome, Jews and proselytes,

11. Cretes and Arabians, we do hear them speak in our tongues the wonderful works of God.

12. And they were all amazed, and were in doubt, saying one to another, What meaneth this?

13. Others mocking said, These men are full of new wine.

BIBLICAL DEFINITIONS

A. Pentecost (Acts 2:1) *pentekoste* (Gk.)—A Jewish feast that marks the beginning of harvest activities. It begins on the 50th day, following Passover. For Christians it has come to be known as the day the Holy Spirit descended upon Christ's followers.

B. Holy Ghost (v. 4) *pneuma hagios* (Gk.)—The third person of the Holy Trinity, also called the Holy Spirit.

LIGHT ON THE WORD

The celebration of Pentecost, as depicted in the New Testament (**Acts 2:1–21**), was prophesied in the Old Testament in **Joel 2:28–32**. Many believe that the Day of Pentecost marked the beginning of the Christian church. The celebration united Jews from many nations; 16 nations are mentioned. Filled with and empowered by the Holy Spirit, the apostles, who were Galileans, preached the Gospel to the Jewish nations in the listeners' native languages.

TEACHING THE BIBLE LESSON

LIFE NEED FOR TODAY'S LESSON

AIM: That your students will understand the freedom achieved through the power of the Holy Spirit.

INTRODUCTION
Pentecost

The origin of Pentecost precedes the birth, death, and Resurrection of Jesus Christ. It's one of the seven feasts of Jehovah and one of the three major Pilgrimage Feasts. Pentecost is celebrated fifty days after Passover, on the Sabbath, and was also called the "Feast of Harvest" and the "Feast of First fruits." God presented these holy feasts to Moses, and it was required that the children of Israel observe them annually (**Leviticus 23:5–21**). Pentecost is symbolically related to the Jewish holiday Shavuot or the "Feast of Weeks," which celebrates Moses receiving the Ten Commandments on Mount Sinai. In the New Testament, Pentecost takes on yet another meaning. Christians celebrate Pentecost as a commemoration of the descent of the Holy Spirit and the outpouring of the gifts of the Spirit. The parallel between Shavuot and Pentecost is interesting. Shavuot also represents the Jews being freed from bondage to Egypt, while Pentecost represents humankind being freed from slavery to sin.

BIBLE LEARNING

AIM: That your students will understand the power of agreement to bring the presence of the Holy Spirit.

I. POWER OF AGREEMENT
(Acts 2:1–3)

Imagine you are part of a baseball team that's about to play the tiebreaker in the World Series. It is the moment you've worked for and anticipated. When you arrive at the stadium, you find that your team's pitcher and catcher didn't show up. The team players that are present are panicking and bickering among themselves. Can this team play a winning game? Are they going to win the support of their fans? No, of course not.

The apostles were also a team, with Jesus as their leader. It was vital that God's team be of one accord in body, mind, and spirit on this history-making Day of Pentecost.

Manifestation of the Holy Spirit
(verses 1–3)

1 And when the day of Pentecost was fully come, they were all with one accord in one place. 2 And suddenly there came a sound from heaven as of a rushing mighty wind, and it filled all the house where they were sitting. 3 And there appeared unto them cloven tongues like as of fire, and it sat upon each of them.

There are two important factors that existed on the Day of Pentecost: (1) the apostles were all gathered together in one place, and (2) they were all of one accord. They knew beforehand that this was going to happen, and they were in complete agreement with it as they anticipated the Spirit's advent. Compliance with the Holy Spirit and with each other was necessary for the success of the events that were about to unfold.

The manifestation of the Holy Spirit was not a quiet, natural affair. It was rather an audacious, supernatural event. The Holy Spirit arrived with a loud sound, like that of a strong gust of wind or mighty storm. It was a sound so loud that it filled the place where they were sitting. Its mighty force was heard and felt by everyone there. It's likely that the surrounding area also heard the arrival of the Holy Spirit. However, to signify that this was a supernatural event, the fixation was on this particular place.

The coming of the Holy Spirit on the early Christian church was both audible (the sound of a mighty rushing wind) and visible (appeared as "cloven" [divided] tongues of fire). It must have been an amazing experience. The visible evidence of the presence of the Holy Spirit in the form of what appeared to be flames sat upon all of them—not consuming flames. These flames remind us of the burning bush (**Exodus 3:2–5**). God called to Moses out of a bush that burned but was not consumed. In both cases the unquenchable flames represented the presence of the Spirit of God. But at Pentecost, the flames were not untouchable as in the bush in the wilderness. No one in the house was excluded from this experience. As He is given to all who believe in the Lord Jesus Christ, the Spirit was given to them all.

SEARCH THE SCRIPTURES
QUESTION 1

What appeared to those present in the upper room on the Day of Pentecost?

Tongues of fire fell on them.

LIGHT ON THE WORD
The Gift

When a person receives the gift of salvation, it does not automatically mean that they receive the indwelling of the Holy Spirit. A great example is shown when Paul asked John's disciples, "Have ye received the Holy Ghost since ye believed?" (**Acts 19:2**). However, to have the Holy Spirit move upon men and to be filled with the indwelling of the Holy Spirit are two different things. Prior to the coming of Christ, the Holy Ghost moved upon the prophets, and they did great and mighty works and spoke as oracles of God. After Jesus' death and Resurrection, He breathed upon the apostles to receive the Holy Spirit (**John 20:22**), but the filling or indwelling of the Spirit would take place on Pentecost with the coming of the "promised" Comforter. Upon being filled with the indwelling of the Holy Spirit, the apostles spoke in tongues (**Acts 2:4**), and it caught the attention of a multitude of Jewish people from many lands that had come for the festival. It was especially strange to them because they all heard their own languages being spoken.

II. THE SPIRIT LED LIFE (Acts 2:4–5)

The Holy Spirit guides us in our spiritual walk (**John 16:13**). The more we seek and follow the direction of the Holy Spirit in our lives, the more He is able to use us. The fullness of the Holy Spirit is necessary for us to reach the pinnacle of sanctification. The idea of being filled with the Spirit is one of allowing God to have control. It is as though instead of holding on to the steering wheel, you handed God the keys to the car and agreed to go along for the ride. To be filled with the Spirit requires us to be in submission to God so He can direct our lives and transform us.

Filled With The Holy Spirit (verses 4–5)

4 And they were all filled with the Holy Ghost, and began to speak with other tongues, as the Spirit gave them utterance. 5 And there were dwelling at Jerusalem Jews, devout men, out of every nation under heaven.

Being filled with the Spirit, a repeated experience, is to be distinguished though not disconnected from the baptism of the Spirit, a one-time experience. In the Scriptures, when people were filled with the Spirit, they were enabled to carry out special ministry tasks from the Lord. Here, the filling with the Spirit led to the ability of those gathered in the house to speak with "other tongues." **Verse 4** does not tell us the nature of these tongues, whether they were ecstatic or not. However, the context would suggest that they were known languages, since **verse 6** reports that the people heard them speaking in their own languages. That the disciples were able to speak in these other languages was no less amazing. They spoke by the power of the Holy Spirit. The Jews dwelling at Jerusalem were devout men of every nation under heaven. In the Greek, devout means "reverencing God; pious; religious." Thus, many of the Jews present during this event were pilgrims from other nations who had come to Jerusalem to celebrate Pentecost. That they were from "every nation under heaven" is a way of saying that they were from many different places.

QUESTION 2

What happened when the Holy Spirit fell on those in the Upper Room?

They began to speak in other tongues as the Spirit gave them utterance.

LIGHT ON THE WORD

Empowered for Ministry

When the apostles were filled with the Holy Spirit, it was then that He empowered them with the gifts of the Spirit. Gifts of the Spirit should not be confused with the fruit of the Spirit. Gifts of the Spirit enable us to serve others. The fruit of the Spirit develops and grows throughout our lives. It is measured by the quality of our Christian walk. The more we delve into God's Word and apply its teachings to our lives, the more spiritual growth we experience. The more we grow, the more evident the fruit of the Spirit becomes in our lives. The fruit of the Spirit is love, joy, peace, longsuffering, gentleness, goodness, faith, meekness, and temperance (**Galatians 5:22–23**).

III. MIRACLE OF THE SPIRIT (Acts 2:6–13)

On the Day of Pentecost, the apostles were graced with the gift of speaking in tongues. In this event, these Galileans preached the Gospel of Jesus Christ in the native languages of the Jewish people. This was a miracle, an unexplainable and unlikely event that amazed and confused the crowd, and led them to inquire about this strange occurrence. Perhaps we can compare it to the experience of hearing the performance of a musical savant. A savant may have the mentality of a young child, but he can play the piano like an accomplished composer. When we witness such a thing, we are astonished. It is simply beyond our human comprehension. It's a miracle. So it was on the Day of Pentecost.

Empowered by the Spirit (verses 6–13)

6 Now when this was noised abroad, the multitude came together, and were confounded, because that every man heard them speak in his own language. 7 And they were all amazed and marvelled, saying one to another, Behold, are not all these which speak Galilaeans? 8 And how hear we every man in our own tongue, wherein we were born? 9 Parthians, and Medes, and Elamites, and the dwellers in Mesopotamia, and in Judaea, and Cappadocia, in Pontus, and Asia, 10 Phrygia, and Pamphylia, in Egypt, and in the parts of Libya about Cyrene, and strangers of Rome, Jews and proselytes, 11 Cretes and Arabians, we do hear them speak in our tongues the wonderful works of God. 12 And they were all amazed, and were in doubt, saying one to another, What meaneth this? 13 Others mocking said, These men are full of new wine.

The noise of the arrival of the Holy Spirit was very loud and drew a great crowd from those who had come to Jerusalem for the Jewish celebration of Pentecost. The people were "astonished" which means they were stirred up. Some may have been thrown into disorder while others were blessed and amazed. Many did not understand what was happening, and they were very vocal about their confusion. Some of them understood Aramaic, the language that the disciples spoke, and others understood Greek, the language spoken by the educated people of that day. But no language speaks to us about spiritual things like the language spoken in our homes as we were growing up. And this is what the multitude heard. They came from many faraway places and spoke many different languages, but they could hear the disciples speaking in the languages that touched their hearts. All the apostles were from the region of Galilee, just as Jesus was. Not only were they speakers of Aramaic, but they had their own distinctive accent. Just as an American can tell a Texan from a Bostonian, so those who lived in Jerusalem could tell that the apostles were from Galilee, just by listening to how they spoke Aramaic. Those from the region of Galilee were mostly humble village people, without cosmopolitan knowledge of a variety of languages.

Most of the people in this crowd were descendants of Jews who had been taken away when the Northern Kingdom (Israel) was defeated by the Assyrians and those who were taken away when the Southern Kingdom (Judea) was defeated by the Babylonians. The Parthians, Medes, and Elamites came from what is modern day Iran. They were also known earlier as Persians or Medo-Persians. This was the farthest east to which the Roman Empire stretched. Then, to the North of Jerusalem were Cappadocia and Pontus, which were part of the Roman province of Asia (just a small part of the Asian continent). Moving to the West were Phrygia and Pamphylia. All these, except for Pamphylia, were located in the Roman province of Asia, now in modern day Turkey. However, the people in those days were not Turkish. The Turks moved in at a much later date. And then, to the South of Israel is Africa. Philo, himself a Jew from Alexandria, estimated that there were a million Jews living in Alexandria alone. Jewish people from Egypt (Alexandria) and Cyrene (a city located in modern day Libya) came to participate in Pentecost. This is almost like Babel coming undone. Although these people came to Jerusalem for the Jewish holiday of Pentecost, the mother tongues represented here came from the east, north, west, and south. It was no accident of history that the Holy Spirit came down upon God's people in a dramatic fashion when people from everywhere known to the people of that day were gathered together in Jerusalem.

Also, there were proselytes in the groups (Gentiles who had been converted to Judaism). Those who were gathered were amazed to hear these people speaking in their own languages, especially in light of the fact that the speakers were all Galileans and not from any of the lands whose languages they spoke. They heard these believers speaking of the mighty acts of God, which no doubt included His former acts of old and His new ones accomplished in the person and work of Jesus Christ. Such an amazing miracle needed an explanation. Thus, the amazed and perplexed bystanders ask, "What does this mean?" No matter how amazing the miracles, there are always skeptics, those who question the veracity of God's acts, and always those who ridicule God's work. So it was in this case. There were those who jeered at or derided the event, attributing God's miracle to the effects of alcohol. They accused those whom God had filled with the Spirit of being drunk with wine.

QUESTION 3

In an attempt to explain away the miracle, what did the mockers in the crowds say about the apostles?

The apostles were drunk with wine.

BIBLE APPLICATION

AIM: That your students will be empowered by the Holy Spirit to join God in His work.

Move Out By The Holy Spirit

There are so many hurting people in today's world. Homelessness, poverty, illness, addiction, violence, injustice, and loneliness are just a few of the problems that plague our society. Even Christians can be overwhelmed when we look around and see all the suffering and need. It would be easier to stick our heads in the sand and let someone else deal with it, and many people do just that. Remember that the Holy Spirit empowers us to come out of our comfort zones and to reach out and help others.

STUDENTS' RESPONSES

AIM: That your students will ask the Holy Spirit to call them to action in their communities.

The empowerment of the Holy Spirit is at work in faithful hearts, to reach out to lost, hurting souls and unite a community. When you look around your community, what do you see? Who is hurting, who needs help, and who needs to hear the Gospel of Jesus Christ? There are so many. Are you going to answer the Holy Spirit's call to action, or are you going to leave the burden for someone else?

PRAYER

Father, we thank You for the power and presence of the Holy Spirit in the church and in each of us individually to represent You in the earth. We pray for You to infill us continually to impact the world for Your glory and to bring Your kingdom on earth as it is in heaven. We pray that those who don't know You will receive the truth of the Gospel and the blessing of Your Holy Spirit. In Jesus' name, we pray. Amen.

DIG A LITTLE DEEPER

Jesus *promised* the disciples a comforter in John

16 that would guide them into all truth, reprove the world of sin, and glorify Christ in the life of the believer. In Acts 1:8, Jesus promised the disciples they would have the power to become His witnesses throughout a progressively expanding circle. Believers today have the same promise of a comforter that gives them the power to live victoriously here on earth. We see the fulfillment of Acts 1:8 because the church that started in Jerusalem is now worldwide. The disciples then had to exhibit *patience* as they waited on the promise to be fulfilled. The passion and resurrection of Christ happened during Passover and the Feast of First Fruits. The disciples were now in the fifty-day period until the Festival of Weeks. Jesus' ascension took place on the fortieth day, and the disciples were told to wait until the power came. Any believer who is seeking the Holy Ghost should wait on the promise in full expectation to be filled. On the fiftieth day, the Holy Ghost came in full *performance* through sound, sight, and touch. Even today the infilling of the Holy Ghost results in speaking in tongues and the life lived demonstrates the fruit of the Spirit.

HOW TO SAY IT

Parthians.   PAR-thee-uhnz.

Elamites.   EE-luh-mites.

Mesopotamia.   mess-o-po-TAY-mih-uh. Cappadocia.   kap-ih-DOH-shee-uh.

Phrygia.   FRIH-dzih-uh.

Pamphylia.   pam-FIhL-ih-uh.

Cyrene.   sigh-REE-neh.

Proselytes.   PRAH-suh-lites.

DAILY HOME BIBLE READINGS

MONDAY
I Will Not Leave You Orphaned
(John 14:18–24)

TUESDAY
Abide in Me
(John 15:1–7)

WEDNESDAY
The Coming of the Advocate
(John 16:1–11)

THURSDAY
Raised Up and Freed from Death
(Acts 2:22–28)

FRIDAY
The Promise of the Spirit
(Acts 2:14–21)

SATURDAY
The Promise Received
(Acts 2:29–36)

SUNDAY
The Day of Pentecost
(Acts 2:1–13)

PREPARE FOR NEXT SUNDAY

Read **1 Thessalonians 4:13-5:11**, and study "Living with Hope."

Sources:
Aharoni, Yohanan, and Michael Avi-Yonah. The Mac- millan Bible Atlas. Revised edition. New York, NY: Macmillan Publishing Company, 1977.
Biblical Words Pronunciation Guide. http://netministries.org/Bbasics/bwords.htm (accessed November 3, 2011).
Bruce, F. F. Commentary on the Book of the Acts. The New International Commentary on the New Testament. Grand Rapids, MI: Wm. B. Eerdmans Publishing Co., 1983.
Beitzel, Barry J. The Moody Atlas of Bible Lands. Chicago, IL: Moody Press, 1985.
Merriam-Webster Online Dictionary. http://www. merriam-webster.com (accessed November 3, 2011).
New Testament Greek Lexicon. http://www.biblestudy-tools.com/lexicons/greek (accessed October 31, 2011). Pfeiffer, Charles F., Howard F. Vos, and John Rea, eds.
Wycliffe Bible Dictionary. Peabody, MA: Hendrick- son Publishers, 2001.

HOPE COMES FROM GOD'S GRACE

BIBLE BASIS: 2 Thessalonians 2:1–3, 9–17

BIBLE TRUTH: Paul warns us against the deception that can come from satanic sources.

MEMORY VERSE: "Now our Lord Jesus Christ himself, and God, even our Father, which hath loved us, and hath given us everlasting consolation and good hope through grace, Comfort your hearts, and stablish you in every good word and work" (2 Thessalonians 2:16-17, KJV).

LESSON AIM: By the end of the lesson, we will: EXPLORE the purpose for which God has called us; TRUST that God has a significant plan for our lives; and PRAY for a clear understanding of God's assignment.

BACKGROUND SCRIPTURES: 2 Thessalonians 2, KJV — Read and incorporate the insights gained from the Background Scriptures into your study of the lesson.

TEACHER PREPARATION

MATERIALS NEEDED: Bibles, (several different versions), Quarterly Commentary/Teacher Manual, Adult Quarterly, teaching resources such as charts, worksheets/handouts, paper, pens, and pencils.

OTHER MATERIALS NEEDED / TEACHER'S NOTES:

_____

_____

LESSON OVERVIEW

LIFE NEED FOR TODAY'S LESSON

That your students will remember that God has called us to make a difference to a lost and dying world.

BIBLE LEARNING

To understand how we need to be intentional in living our lives for God.

BIBLE APPLICATION

To appreciate the importance of becoming children of a holy God.

STUDENTS' RESPONSES

Students will develop ways to discern the difference between God's Word and false teachings.

LESSON SCRIPTURE

2 THESSALONIANS 2:1–3, 9–17, KJV

1. Now we beseech you, brethren, by the coming of our Lord Jesus Christ, and by our gathering together unto him,

2. That ye be not soon shaken in mind, or be troubled, neither by spirit, nor by word, nor by letter as from us, as that the day of Christ is at hand.

3. Let no man deceive you by any means: for that day shall not come, except there come a falling away first, and that man of sin be revealed, the son of perdition;

2:9. Even him, whose coming is after the working of Satan with all power and signs and lying wonders,

10. And with all deceivableness of unrighteousness in them that perish; because they received not the love of the truth, that they might be saved.

11. And for this cause God shall send them strong delusion, that they should believe a lie:

12. That they all might be damned who be- lieved not the truth, but had pleasure in un- righteousness.

13. But we are bound to give thanks alway to God for you, brethren beloved of the Lord, because God hath from the beginning chosen you to salvation through sanctification of the Spirit and belief of the truth:

14. Whereunto he called you by our gospel, to the obtaining of the glory of our Lord Jesus Christ.

15. Therefore, brethren, stand fast, and hold the traditions which ye have been taught, whether by word, or our epistle.

16. Now our Lord Jesus Christ himself, and God, even our Father, which hath loved us, and hath given us everlasting consolation and good hope through grace,

17. Comfort your hearts, and stablish you in every good word and work.

BIBLICAL DEFINITIONS

A. Bound (2 Thessalonians 2:13) *opheilo* (Gk)—Under obligation.
B. Salvation (v.13) *soteria* (G_k.)—Rescue, deliverance from danger or sin.

C. Sanctification (v.13) *hagiasmos* (Gk.)—State of purity, holiness.

LIGHT ON THE WORD
False Teachings

Paul, Silas, and Timothy founded the church at Thessalonica on Paul's second missionary journey (**Acts 17:1–10**), but the Apostle Paul had to leave in a hurry because of the degree of persecution there. In Paul's first letter to the church, he not only comforted these struggling believers, but also offered encouragement because they were still experiencing threats and other harassment for their faith in Almighty God. However, false teachings were also causing problems for this infant church because incorrect information about Jesus' second coming spread and caused some to quit their jobs and become idle. Idleness bred the sinful conduct of busybodies, minding other people's business.

TEACHING THE BIBLE LESSON

LIFE NEED FOR TODAY'S LESSON

AIM: That your students will encourage persons to study and know God's Word so they can correct false teachings.

INTRODUCTION
Deception and False Teachers

Not too long ago, a rich Christian-professing man announced via radio spots, billboards, etc. that the rapture was going to happen, and he gave a date for it. Many non-Christians made fun of him, especially as the date passed and nothing happened. How could a careful reading of today's Scripture passage help us not to be deceived by such messages? Do you know other Scriptures that would also show that this prophecy was wrong? How can true Christians avoid causing people to laugh at the cause of Christ?

BIBLE LEARNING

AIM: That your students will not be deceived by false teachers.

I. THOSE NOT LEFT BEHIND (2 Thessalonians 2:1-3)

Most Bible scholars identify the "man of sin" in today's Scripture passage as identical to an antichrist written about by John (**2 Thessalonians 2:3**). In his epistles, John describes this antichrist as denying the incarnation (**1 John 4:3; 2 John 7**), and denying the deity of Christ (**1 John 2:2**). The incarnation is the theological term for the Son of God becoming a human being. Deity is the truth that Jesus was and is truly God. These two truths taken together show us that Jesus was both fully human and fully God. To deny these two central truths is to be an antichrist. While there is a generic description of an antichrist, Scripture tells us that there will be a specific figure with great influence who will be the ultimate Antichrist.

Antichrist (verses 1–3)

1 Now we beseech you, brethren, by the coming of our Lord Jesus Christ, and by our gathering together unto him, 2 That ye be not soon shaken in mind, or be troubled, neither by spirit, nor by word, nor by letter as from us, as that the day of Christ is at hand. 3 Let no man deceive you by any means: for that day shall not come, except there come a falling away first, and that man of sin be revealed, the son of perdition;

The Fake Letter (verses 1–3)

It is presumed, someone either spoke on behalf of or had forged a letter that was supposed to have come from Paul. They said that the day of the Lord had already come. Many novelists, motivational speakers, so-called spiritual leaders, and even a few contemporary preachers have given people information that is contrary to what the Bible teaches concerning the second coming of our Lord. Some have even claimed to be the Messiah.

But Paul quickly spoke to comfort the Thessalonian Christians confirming—Jesus has not yet returned. The Bible gives us many warning signs. Among the signs is the coming of the man of sin or lawlessness, also called an antichrist, the ultimate of whom we can read about in **Revelation 13**. At this time, there will be open rebellion against God. So no, Jesus has not yet returned. And we do not need to worry about being left behind if we have accepted Jesus Christ as our Savior.

SEARCH THE SCRIPTURES

QUESTION 1

Why did Paul warn them not to be "shaken in their mind or be troubled" about Jesus' return?

Paul warned them not be shaken or troubled because the information they received that Jesus had returned was not true and that the man of sin had to first be revealed before Jesus' return.

LIGHT ON THE WORD

The Beast and The Antichrist

In **Revelation 13:1–8**, the description of the beast is often equated with the antichrist and the false prophet. Jesus also mentioned false Christs (**Matthew 24:24; Mark 13:22**). The antichrist is prophesied to come right before the great tribulation occurs. Some theologians interpret the antichrist or false prophet symbolically, i.e., a spirit of unbelief.

II. THOSE FOOLED BY THE MAN OF SIN (1 Thessalonians 2:9–12)

Many erudite Bible scholars are not sure how to interpret some of the verses in today's passage (especially if they do not have the Holy Ghost).

In fact, all people struggle with things spiritually discerned when researching it with a carnal mind. For instance, many are not sure if the man of sin is an individual or an organization. But we know that the false prophet is a man. The antichrist spirit is both man and institution. We also know that Satan is limited, and can only do what God allows him to do. Even now he is being restrained, but shortly before the Lord returns, God will let go of the restraints, and he will be free to do more evil than we could imagine.

Be Not Deceived (verses 9–12)

9 Even him, whose coming is after the working of Satan with all power and signs and lying wonders, 10 And with all deceivableness of unrighteousness in them that perish; because they received not the love of the truth, that they might be saved. 11 And for this cause God shall send them strong delusion, that they should believe a lie: 12 That they all might be damned who believed not the truth, but had pleasure in unrighteousness.

These verses continue the conversation concerning the man of sin. Again we see that Satan is behind him. The word "all" means every ungodly "power and sign and lying wonder." "Lying" also means intentionally false, and here it also modifies power, signs, and wonders. So the man of sin seems able to do great wonders, but they are all shams. The sad thing is that those who have rejected Jesus Christ will not be able to see how false all these wonders are. They will be lured into deeper falsehood. We see followers of false religions today who seem oblivious to how deceitful these religions are.

QUESTION 2

What is God's response to those who "did not receive the love of the truth"?

God will send very strong forms of deception

their way because they believed "a lie."

LIGHT ON THE WORD

The Cost of Rejecting the Lord

Despite the evil Satan represents, those who have rejected the Lord will believe in him. The word "delusion" means fraudulence, a straying from orthodoxy or piety, delusion, deceit, or error. This delusion is the man of sin and all he represents. However, those who follow the Lamb will not be deceived.

III. LOVED, CHOSEN, AND CALLED (2 Thessalonians 2:13–14)

In today's passage, **2 Thessalonians 2:14**, Paul reiterated that God worked through Silas, Timothy, and himself to bring the Good News of salvation to the Thessalonians. Still, their salvation was all about God and His work and not about Paul and his companions, who apart from God's work are like us. Yet, God can and does take fallible, unfaithful, untrustworthy human beings and use them for His glory.

Giving Thanks to God Regardless (verse 13–14)

13 But we are bound to give thanks alway to God for you, brethren beloved of the Lord, because God hath from the beginning chosen you to salvation through sanctification of the Spirit and belief of the truth: 14 Whereunto he called you by our gospel, to the obtaining of the glory of our Lord Jesus Christ.

In this second letter to the Thessalonians, Paul reaffirmed that he and his companions (Silas and Timothy, the founders of the church at Thessalonica) were "bound," which means "under obligation, indebted," to always give thanks to God for these believers. They felt bound because God had from the beginning of the world "chosen" these believers to become a part of His family and had used Paul, Silas, and

Timothy to bring them the Good News. In other words, God chose to save the Thessalonians. The word "salvation" means "rescue, deliverance, preservation, and saving." God chose to rescue these Thessalonians from the power of sin and the penalty of sin, which is death (that is, eternal separation from a holy God). It is also God at work, through His Holy Spirit, who used "sanctification," meaning "consecration, purification," to make the Thessalonians holy as He is holy. Their salvation had been all about God doing a work by or through them. God, by His power, is transforming them from sinners to believers. One of His attributes is He is omnipotent (all-powerful). He used that power to bring the Thessalonians into His fold.

QUESTION 3

How often does Paul say to the "beloved" to give thanks to God and who are the beloved?

Always[s]; Silas and Timothy, his companions, and founders of the church at Thessalonica.

LIGHT ON THE WORD
God's Invitation

Paul also reaffirmed to the Thessalonians that God "called" or "invited, named," them out of sin to salvation. He used the Good News of salvation—the Gospel—His Word—to save them. They believed upon the Lord Jesus Christ and were delivered from sin, and from eternal or everlasting damnation (**John 3:16**). Their salvation brought "glory" or "honor, praise, worship, splendor, excellence" to almighty God. When they were saved, they, too, became a part of His kingdom that will reign forever and ever.

IV. STANDING FIRM IN THE FAITH (2 Thessalonians 2:15–17)

After encouraging the Thessalonians in the faith, Paul cautioned them to "stand fast, and hold the traditions, which ye have been taught." The phrase "stand fast" means "to stand firm, to persevere, to persist" in the faith. They were to hold to the traditions that they had been taught when they first believed. The word "hold" is "to use strength, lay hold on, be master of." They were to hold onto, seize, and retain those fundamentals of the faith that they had been first taught. They were not to grab hold of false doctrine concerning Jesus' second coming and become idle in their daily living. This false doctrine contradicted the principles that Paul had taught them that his life had embodied before them.

Stand Fast (verses 15–17)

15 Therefore, brethren, stand fast, and hold the traditions which ye have been taught, whether by word, or our epistle. 16 Now our Lord Jesus Christ himself, and God, even our Father, which hath loved us, and hath given us everlasting consolation and good hope through grace, 17 Comfort your hearts, and stablish you in every good word and work.

Now that Paul had built up the Thessalonians by encouraging them in the faith, he moved on to encourage them to stand firm in their faith. He wanted them to commit to faithfulness to God, who was more than enough in their times of troubles. The apostle knew that one threat to the church was false teaching or doctrine. Just as can happen today, falsehoods could cause believers to walk in a way that God does not intend for them to walk. For the Thessalonians, believing that the Second Coming was imminent had caused them to fall into the sins of idleness and being busybodies (meddling into other people's affairs). Of course, a lost and dying world saw this idleness and confusion in the church. This was indeed a negative witness. It did not represent the holy God well. Paul, therefore, urged them to commit and hold on to the foundational truths that they had been taught from the beginning of their faith and get back to work.

In **verses 16** and **17**, Paul ended this part of his letter by reminding the Thessalonians that it was God who loved them and has done so with His special favor ("grace"); this same God gave them "everlasting consolation" and hope through salvation by believing in Jesus Christ. According to **John 10:28**, Jesus said, "And I give unto them eternal life; and they shall never perish, neither shall any man pluck them out of my hand." This means that Jesus protects believers from harm forever and ever. All believers can expect to suffer here on earth. Yet we have the assurance from God Himself that Satan cannot harm our souls or take away our eternal life that Jesus paid for in full when He died on the Cross. Paul then prayed that this same God would both comfort the Thessalonians' hearts in the midst of their struggles as well as give them strength in everything that they did and said.

QUESTION 4

Paul shares that there is an "everlasting" special blessing that we have from God in the form of "good hope" through_____.

grace.

LIGHT ON THE WORD
Study God's Word

Because of false teachers and doctrines, it is really important that believers, even today, study God's Word in context, cross-referencing Scriptures in order to know what the Bible actually says or teaches. Bible study requires knowledge of context, which means that we should not just read a given Scripture verse and draw our own conclusions. Instead, we should read the Scriptures surrounding the text; for example, look at the entire chapter; then, look at the book the chapter is contained in. Finally, we should see if our interpretation of that Scripture contradicts what the Bible teaches as a whole. Also, consider the people, places, and times of that Scripture. What was happening at the time? All these things bring clarity to the meaning.

BIBLE APPLICATION

AIM: That your students will begin to understand that standing firm on God's Word through Jesus Christ is essential to growing in their relationship faith.

Listening to God's Voice

John and Mary saw that there was still much work to be done at their church, located in the heart of an inner city neighborhood. They had been members in good standing for more than 25 years, had seen several pastors come and go to greener pastures, and had witnessed firsthand the financial, personal, and spiritual struggles of the church. It was more than tempting for John and Mary to throw in the towel, too, and attend the beautiful suburban church near their home. Both had studied God's Word at a major theological institution and could have easily gone to other, more stable churches to share their knowledge of God's inerrant Word. However, one day as John studied the Scriptures, he ran across a passage in Luke's Gospel: "But their scribes and Pharisees murmured against his disciples, saying, Why do ye eat and drink with publicans and sinners? And Jesus answering said unto them, They that are whole need not a physician; but they that are sick. I came not to call the righteous, but sinners to repentance" (**Luke 5:30–32**). This signifies that one cannot reach and win the loss without communication.

John realized that everyone called to salvation may not be chosen to serve in the church. God does equip the called through His Holy Spirit to work. At first, some may not appear to have it all together—thriving spiritually and physically but they eventually grow in both grace of God, and knowledge of His will. God uses workers in churches that understand struggling—they can reach people that truly need the Physician, God.

John felt convicted. He knew that the Lord had him and Mary still in their present church's vineyard because there were many who were spiritually sick and needed to be taught God's Word.

STUDENTS' RESPONSES

AIM: That your students will learn where and how God wants them to work in building His kingdom on earth.

PRAYER

Dear Awesome God, we praise You and honor Your name for allowing us to worship You and to share the goodness of who You are with others. Keep us focused on Jesus and all that You want us to do here on earth as we serve others and care for all of Your creation. In Jesus' name, we pray. Amen.

DIG A LITTLE DEEPER

In April 1968 when Civil Rights icon Martin Luther King was assassinated, one of his lieutenants, the Rev. Jesse Jackson, tried to rally despairing and disillusioned activists and their communities with the slogan, "keep hope alive." Although Jackson and others believed that continuing protests, combined with full participation in local and national elections, would keep producing positive change, statistics indicate that hope decreased and hopelessness increased during the five decades since King's death. Although most African Americans are now classified as middle class, some are among the world's billionaires, and a record number have been elected to public office since the mid-20th century, hopelessness among African Americans has increased. Why has this happened? Is it because apparent wealth has disguised a reality of economic vulnerability? Has "mass incarceration" undermined community and crippled the family? Or is the increase in hopelessness the product of another

source? Was the hope for a better future – for the promised land of King's famous dream – based on faith in the United States' legal, political, and economic systems? Were leaders and followers satisfied with more "seats at the table" of American prosperity? Or was this hope, Jackson referred to, based on faith in the promises of God and a willingness to obey the commandments of Jesus Christ?

Paul reminded believers in Thessalonica that their hope was grounded in Jesus' love for them and that by His grace He would comfort and encourage them to continue doing good works and to share the promises of God with others. Their hope was based on their belief that God's kingdom would be established even though they were suffering because of their faith. Paul reminded them that they will be blessed if they hold on to "the values, ethos, and traditions of the Lord Jesus" (*Fortress Commentary on the Bible: The New Testament*, 2014, p. 586). Can God's grace "keep hope alive" for contemporary African Americans, so many of whom appear to be "drunk with the wine of the world" and, as a result, to have forgotten God? What does the warning against doing so, written over a hundred years ago by James Weldon Johnson for the hymn, "Lift Every Voice and Sing," mean for African Americans today? Is it possible to "keep hope alive" by renewing faith in Jesus Christ and depending even more on God's "amazing grace"?

HOW TO SAY IT

Perdition.	per-DIH-shun.
Incarnation.	in-kar-NAY-shun.
Consolation.	kahn-suh-LAY-shun.

74

DAILY HOME BIBLE READINGS

MONDAY
An Appointed Time
(Psalm 75)

TUESDAY
The Day Is Coming
(Malachi 4)

WEDNESDAY
No Good Thing Withheld
(Psalm 84)

THURSDAY
My Help Comes from the Lord
(Psalm 121)

FRIDAY
The Hope of Eternal Life
(Titus 3:1-7)

SATURDAY
Kept Sound and Blameless
(1 Thessalonians 5:23-28)

SUNDAY
Eternal Comfort and Good Hope
(2 Thessalonians 2:1-3, 9-17)

PREPARE FOR NEXT SUNDAY

Read **1 Peter 1:3-12** and study "A Living Hope."

Sources:

Best, Ernest. A Commentary on the First and Second Epistles to the Thessalonians. New York, NY: Harper and Row Publishers, 1972.

Henry, Matthew. Commentary on the Whole Bible. Edited by Leslie F. Church, et al. Grand Rapids, MI: Zondervan, 1961. 1884-1885.

Life Application Study Bible (New Living Translation). Wheaton, IL: Tyndale House, 1996. 1923.

Merriam-Webster Online Dictionary. http://www. merriam-webster.com (accessed November 3, 2011).

New Testament Greek Lexicon. http://www.biblestu- dytools.com/lexicons/greek (accessed October 31, 2011).

Vincent, Marvin R. Word Studies in the New Testa- ment. Grand Rapids, MI: Wm. B. Eerdmans Publish- ing Co., 1957.

COMMENTS / NOTES:

A LIVING HOPE

BIBLE BASIS: 1 Peter 1:3–12

BIBLE TRUTH: Peter focuses our attention on the resurrection of Jesus Christ.

MEMORY VERSE: "Blessed be the God and Father of our Lord Jesus Christ, which according to his abundant mercy hath begotten us again unto a lively hope by the resurrection of Jesus Christ from the dead" (1 Peter 1:3, KJV).

LESSON AIM: By the end of the lesson, we will: KNOW how we can find meaning in life's challenges; FEEL the hope of Christ and be able to share that hope with others; and ACTIVELY turn to Christ for hope and guidance.

BACKGROUND SCRIPTURES: 1 Peter 1:1–12 KJV — Read and incorporate the insights gained from the Background Scriptures into your study of the lesson.

TEACHER PREPARATION

MATERIALS NEEDED: Bibles, (several different versions), Quarterly Commentary/Teacher Manual, Adult Quarterly, teaching resources such as charts, worksheets/handouts, paper, pens, and pencils.

OTHER MATERIALS NEEDED / TEACHER'S NOTES:

_____

_____

LESSON OVERVIEW

LIFE NEED FOR TODAY'S LESSON

To know that hope in Jesus Christ keeps us focused on God.

BIBLE LEARNING

The resurrection of Christ is the promise that we will be raised as well with Christ.

BIBLE APPLICATION

To appreciate the blessings God has given us through Jesus.

STUDENTS' RESPONSES

Students will plan ways to be thankful for the joy that we receive in knowing that our hope in Jesus is everlasting.

LESSON SCRIPTURE

1 PETER 1:3–12, KJV

3. Blessed be the God and Father of our Lord Jesus Christ, which according to his abundant mercy hath begotten us again unto a lively hope by the resurrection of Jesus Christ from the dead,

4. To an inheritance incorruptible, and undefiled, and that fadeth not away, reserved in heaven for you,

5. Who are kept by the power of God through faith unto salvation ready to be revealed in the last time.

6. Wherein ye greatly rejoice, though now for a season, if need be, ye are in heaviness through manifold temptations:

7. That the trial of your faith, being much more precious than of gold that perisheth, though it be tried with fire, might be found unto praise and honour and glory at the ap- pearing of Jesus Christ:

8. Whom having not seen, ye love; in whom, though now ye see him not, yet believing, ye rejoice with joy unspeakable and full of glory:

9. Receiving the end of your faith, even the salvation of your souls.

10. Of which salvation the prophets have en- quired and searched diligently, who prophe- sied of the grace that should come unto you:

11. Searching what, or what manner of time the Spirit of Christ which was in them did signi- fy, when it testified beforehand the sufferings of Christ, and the glory that should follow.

12. Unto whom it was revealed, that not unto themselves, but unto us they did minister the things, which are now reported unto you by them that have preached the gospel unto you with the Holy Ghost sent down from heaven; which things the angels desire to look into.

BIBLICAL DEFINITIONS

A. Lively hope (1 Peter 1:3) *anagennao* (Gk.)— An eternal assurance grounded in the resurrec- tion of Christ; a new birth.
B. Inheritance (v. 4) *kleroo* (Gk.)— Something, as a quality, characteristic, or other immaterial possession, received from progenitors or prede- cessors.

LIGHT ON THE WORD

There is little doubt that the Apostle Peter is the author of this epistle. He introduces himself as such in verse one. We also note that he is writing to strangers (perhaps Greek converts) in various regions of Asia. Whether Peter directed his letter to a specific group or not, it is a matter of encouragement to all Christians who believe in the Lord Jesus Christ, even those of us today who have accepted the truth of the death, burial, and resurrection of Jesus, our Savior. With these motivational words, we are assured there is victory over suffering.

TEACHING THE BIBLE LESSON

LIFE NEED FOR TODAY'S LESSON

AIM: That your students will share the hope they have with those who are in hopeless situations.

INTRODUCTION

Peter Provides Comfort

The Apostle Peter wrote **1 Peter** to Jewish Christians who were driven out of Jerusalem and scattered throughout Asia Minor. There is much that we, too, can learn from his letter.

He wrote to encourage these suffering Chris- tians who were under persecution. Peter was very familiar with persecution himself as he had been beaten and jailed and had been threatened often as he brought God's message to the people. He had also witnessed firsthand not only fellow Christians dying for the faith, but many being scattered as they sought refuge from persecution. Thus, the church was suffering and the Apostle Peter sought to bring comfort and hope to them.

BIBLE LEARNING

AIM: That your students will know that we can find meaning in life's challenges.

77

I. HOPE THROUGH SALVATION (1 Peter 1:3–6)

The Apostle Peter wrote **1 Peter** to believers living in northwestern Asia Minor, known today as Turkey. The bearer of the letter lists the provinces of Pontus, Galatia, Cappadocia, Asia, and Bithynia in the order of visit. Though Peter's ministry was mainly oriented to the Jews, the letter here was addressed to Christians who were largely Gentiles.

The beginning of this section focused on thanksgiving was a Jewish pattern of writing adopted by the Christians. While the Jewish thanksgiving formula is limited to the mention of God, Christian thanksgiving is expanded in identifying God more specifically because of the revelation of Jesus Christ as Lord. Here Peter's praises go to God, the Father of our Lord Jesus Christ. Paul uses the same template for his letters (see **2 Corinthians 1:3; Ephesians 1:3**). This thanksgiving is rooted in what God has accomplished for Peter and his readers.

Hope by the Resurrection of Jesus (verses 3–6)

3 Blessed be the God and Father of our Lord Jesus Christ, which according to his abundant mercy hath begotten us again unto a lively hope by the resurrection of Jesus Christ from the dead, 4 To an inheritance incorruptible, and undefiled, and that fadeth not away, reserved in heaven for you, 5 Who are kept by the power of God through faith unto salvation ready to be revealed in the last time. 6 Wherein ye greatly rejoice, though now for a season, if need be, ye are in heaviness through manifold temptations:

God in His mercy has given new birth to both Peter and the recipient of his letter. In **1 Peter 1:3**, the phrase "a lively hope" is new birth. The concept of the new birth is found in John where the new birth is not dependent on the will of man but that of the Spirit (**1:13; 3:6**). This new birth came through God's mercy and loving-kindness. This new birth reminds the readers that the provision for the new birth is solely the work of God without any merit whatsoever from the receiver of the new birth.

When Adam and Eve sinned against God in the Garden of Eden, man fell from a great estate. This did not catch God by surprise, for He had a plan of redemption already in place. As we read in these two verses, God has already established reconciliation with humankind through the death, burial, and resurrection of our Lord and Savior Jesus Christ. It is through God's abundant mercy that we are not consumed.

The shed blood of Jesus not only brings hope of eternal life, but a "lively hope" to all humankind. Peter writes in **1 Peter 2:5** of Saints being "lively stones" (emphasis added). This dynamic combination of a "lively hope" and "lively stones" allows us to have victory over the cares of this world. We have been translated into Christ's kingdom through the incorruptible inheritance we have received. All of this is accomplished by the resurrection power that is in us through the precious gift of the Holy Ghost. As believers, we have victory over suffering. We have a spiritual heritage built upon an everlasting foundation.

When the entire world is falling apart, our prayer can be: "Let your kingdom come on earth as it is in heaven." We are in this world, but not of it. We serve the God of Abraham, Isaac, and Jacob. It was Abraham who searched for that city that was not made by hand. Through Jesus Christ, we have inherited the promise of His kingdom here on earth. Eternal life will not fade away, for heaven belongs to His Saints.

The importance of faith is found in **verses 5–6**. Remember the song that many congregations used to sing? "Faith, faith, faith, just a little bit of faith. You don't need a whole lot; just use what you got, faith, faith, faith, just a little bit of faith." There is so much truth to that little tune. Jesus taught that all you need is faith the size of a mustard seed, and mountains will move at your command (**Matthew 17:20**).

Peter is encouraging the reader that although there are manifold temptations, we are kept by the power of God through faith. Salvation begins by faith, and we must hold onto faith until that day when we reach our heavenly reward. Perhaps, like Job, you have been considered by God to go through hardship. Rejoice as the fiery tests and trials engulf you, trusting that God will be with you through it all. Take time to learn what the purposes of these experiences are—they exist to make us, not to break us. They will lead us to a blessed and expected end.

SEARCH THE SCRIPTURES
QUESTION 1

What is the heaviness that weighs people down?

Temptation

LIGHT ON THE WORD
The New Birth
The result of the new birth is also inheritance because inheritance is often linked to the parents' and son's relationship whether by birth or adoption (**Romans 8:16–17**). The inheritance notion is found in the Old Testament with the promise of God to Abraham to give him the land of Canaan. The children of Israel received the land through conquest by Joshua. However, their inheritance was plagued with wars, idolatry, and vices, and by the eroding effect of time.

Unlike the inheritance promised to the Israelites, which was subject to degradation because it was temporal, the inheritance God promised to Christians is not subject to these three plagues. Peter uses three qualifiers in Greek to explain the quality of this inheritance.

It is first "incorruptible" or permanent and cannot suffer corruption or corrosion; then, it is "undefiled," morally pure and cannot be tainted; and last, it will never fade {pass} away being "reserved in heaven"—eternal. This inheritance has been set aside for the readers of **1 Peter.**

II. TRIUMPHANT VICTORY
(1 Peter 1:7–12)
In our devotional reading from the Book of Lamentations, Jeremiah lets us know where to place our hope. "The LORD is my portion, saith my soul; therefore will I hope in him" (**Lamentations 3:24**). It seems nearly unimaginable to grasp what the world does when life's challenges happen to them. We as Saints have the Lord to turn to. We are privileged to be able to go to Him in prayer. He is available to console and comfort us. Who wouldn't serve a God like ours?

The Trial of Your Faith (verses 7–12)
7 That the trial of your faith, being much more precious than of gold that perisheth, though it be tried with fire, might be found unto praise and honour and glory at the appearing of Jesus Christ: 8 Whom having not seen, ye love; in whom, though now ye see him not, yet believing, ye rejoice with joy unspeakable and full of glory: 9 Receiving the end of your faith, even the salvation of your souls. 10 Of which salvation the prophets have enquired and searched diligently, who prophesied of the grace that should come unto you: 11 Searching what, or what manner of time the Spirit of Christ which was in them did signify, when it testified beforehand the sufferings of Christ, and the glory that should follow. 12 Unto whom it was revealed, that not unto themselves, but unto us they did minister the things, which are now reported unto you by them that have preached the gospel unto you with

the Holy Ghost sent down from heaven; which things the angels desire to look into.

Precious trials (verse 7). Can you imagine that 24-karat gold is not worth as much as the trials of your faith? This is what Peter is telling us. To the carnal mind that definitely is foolishness. But to those of us who have been given the mind of Christ, how precious is this teaching! These fiery trials that we endure and overcome are going to be currency with Jesus Christ in His appearance. Surely we want Him to be pleased not only then, but now as well. A wise person has said it's all about attitude and perspective. How we look at a situation makes all the difference. Learn to see things as God sees them. Then, the trials that seem like they're going to take you out will become precious and valuable.

Believing faith (verses 8–9). Peter seems to echo the words of Jesus when He was speaking to Thomas: "Jesus saith unto him, Thomas, because thou hast seen me, thou hast believed: blessed are they that have not seen, and yet have believed" (**John 20:29**). We, too, are in that number—believing, rejoicing with unspeakable joy, and full of glory. The promise of hope has been fulfilled, and we are heirs to the promise.

Better days are coming (verses 10–11). Throughout the Old Testament, prophets and common people alike rested in the promise of hope. They looked forward to a better day when the promised Messiah would destroy the works of man. The list is long and covers thousands of years, but these men, women, and children of faith looked to the future in hope. Present-day Saints have a different vantage point. We have all these things recorded in the Word of God. We also have witness in our inner being that Jesus did just as He said. Our hope is in the glorious resurrected Christ. He has provided triumph over death and suffering. Yes, we have eternal hope.

Angelic Curiosity (verse 12). "What is man, that thou art mindful of him? and the son of man, that thou visitest him? For thou hast made him a little lower than the angels, and hast crowned him with glory and honour" (**Psalm 8:4-5**). Man has a place of honor in God's creation. God breathed life into man and he became a living soul (**Genesis 2:7**). No other creature, angelic or otherwise, can boast of this status. However much the angels may be puzzled at God's decision in creation, we do know that in redemption the angels rejoice when a soul is saved (**Luke 15:10**).

QUESTION 2

What is the test of our faith compared to?

The test of our faith is compared to how fire is used to test gold.

LIGHT ON THE WORD

The Prophet's Role

The prophets were told that they were not the recipients of the grace, but they were serving the believers in Christ that will come. When the prophets talked about these things, they were looking forward to the future beneficiaries. Empowered by the Holy Spirit sent by God, the Father, people have preached the same message that was preached to Peter's readers. This reminds us of Jesus commissioning the disciples to go into the world and preach the Gospel after they have received the Holy Spirit (**Matthew 28:18-20; Mark 16:15; Luke 24:49; Acts 1:8**).

BIBLE APPLICATION

AIM: That your students will better understand that we can only put our hope in Jesus.

Not too long ago, a rich Christian man announced via radio spots, billboards, etc. that the rapture was going to happen, and he gave a date for it. Many non-Christians made fun of him, especially as the date passed and nothing happened. How could a careful reading of today's Scripture passage help us not to be deceived by such messages? Do you know other Scriptures that would also show that this prophecy was wrong? How can Christians avoid causing people to laugh at the cause of Christ?

PRAYER

Dear Heavenly Father, we are humbled by Your love, grace, and mercy to give Your life for ours. Your death and resurrection are blessings beyond more than we can imagine. Thank You for allowing us to know the joy of embracing hope and living hope to encourage one another in our daily lives. In Jesus' name, we pray. Amen.

DIG A LITTLE DEEPER

As Christians we believe that Jesus Christ rose from the dead and we have new eternal life in Him. As Scripture says, "we have been born again to an ever-living hope through the resurrection of Jesus Christ from the dead" (1 Peter 1:3b, *Amplified Bible*). Many non-Christians believe that the man, Jesus, lived but they do not believe that he was raised from the dead and lives eternally as the Son of God. How do we as Christians defend our faith to unbelievers and why are we sure that Jesus Christ really lives? What is our evidence? If we were suffering from the intense persecution endured by the first century believers who read Peter's first letter, how could we hold on to our belief that Jesus lives and that we have eternal life because He lives? Would we be willing to suffer persecution and even an agonizing physical death to defend our faith?

As Peter acknowledged, the believers he wrote to loved and believed in Jesus even though, unlike Peter, they had never seen Him (1 Peter 1:8). The Midwestern state of Missouri has been nicknamed "the Show Me State, to describe the "non-credulous, conservative, and strong character" of its residents. The phrase even appears on the state's license plates. (https://www.worldatlas.com/articles/why-is-missouri-known-as-the-show-me-state.html).

A popular modern American "proverb," "seeing is believing," reinforces an unwillingness to be duped by charlatans who cannot provide evidence of their claims.

In response to this culturally reinforced skepticism, what is our evidence that Christ lives in us and that we have a living hope as "living stones . . . a spiritual house . . . a holy priesthood?" (1 Peter 2:5b). Are today's Christians willing to give up the pleasures of this physical life, if need be, and even to suffer physical death to witness to lost souls? Do we demonstrate a willingness to suffer for Christ's sake as evidence that we have been born again? And when our faith is tried, do we, "rejoice with joy unspeakable and full of glory" (1 Peter 1:8b KJV) to "show" the world that our savior lives in us and our living hope is in our salvation: eternal life with Him?

HOW TO SAY IT

Pontus. PAHN-tuhs.

Galatia. guh-LAY-shih-uh.

Cappadocia. kap-ih-DOH-shee-uh.

Bithynia. bih-THIN-ee-uh.

DAILY HOME BIBLE READINGS

MONDAY
I Have No Help in Me
(Job 6:8-13)

TUESDAY
Days without Hope
(Job 7:1-6)

WEDNESDAY
Will Mortals Live Again?
(Job 14:7-17)

THURSDAY
My Times Are in Your Hands
(Psalm 31:9-16)

FRIDAY
The Lord Preserves the Faithful
(Psalm 31:19-24)

SATURDAY
Hope in God's Faithfulness
(Lamentations 3:19-24)

SUNDAY
New Birth into a Living Hope
(1 Peter 1:3-12)

PREPARE FOR NEXT SUNDAY

Read **2 Peter 1:4-14**, and study "Equipped With Hope."

Sources:

Biblical Words Pronunciation Guide. http://netminis- tries.org/Bbasics/bwords.htm (accessed November

Davids, Peter H. The First Epistle of Peter. Grand Rap- ids, MI: Wm. B. Eerdmans, 1990. 7-9, 50-65.

Marshall, I. Howard. 1 Peter: The IVP New Testament Commentary Series. Downers Grove, IL: InterVar- sity, 1991. 32-48.

McKnight, Scot. 1 Peter: The NIV Application Com- mentary. Grand Rapids, MI: Zondervan, 1996. 23-24, 67-82.

New Testament Greek Lexicon. http://www.biblestu- dytools.com/lexicons/greek (accessed October 31, 2011).

Selwyn, Edward G. The First Epistle of St. Peter: The Greek Text with Introduction, Notes and Essays. 2nd ed. Grand Rapids, MI: Baker Book House, 1947. 121-138.

COMMENTS / NOTES:

EQUIPPED WITH HOPE

BIBLE BASIS: 2 Peter 1:4–14

BIBLE TRUTH: Jesus Christ is the foundation upon which we build our faith and sustain our hope.

MEMORY VERSE: "According as his divine power hath given unto us all things that pertain unto life and godliness, through the knowledge of him that hath called us to glory and virtue" (2 Peter 1:3, KJV).

LESSON AIM: By the end of the lesson, we will: EXPLORE biblical ways to lead a more fruitful life; FEEL empowered to live effective and fruitful lives; and DEVELOP a deeper knowledge of the Lord Jesus Christ.

BACKGROUND SCRIPTURES: 2 Peter 1, KJV — Read and incorporate the insights gained from the Background Scriptures into your study of the lesson.

TEACHER PREPARATION

MATERIALS NEEDED: Bibles, (several different versions), Quarterly Commentary/Teacher Manual, Adult Quarterly, teaching resources such as charts, worksheets/handouts, paper, pens, and pencils.

OTHER MATERIALS NEEDED / TEACHER'S NOTES:

_____

_____

LESSON OVERVIEW

LIFE NEED FOR TODAY'S LESSON

To know that hope in Jesus Christ keeps us focused on God.

BIBLE LEARNING

To explore biblical ways to lead a more fruitful life.

BIBLE APPLICATION

To understand why choosing to live an effective life for Christ is important.

STUDENTS' RESPONSES

Students will commit to seeking ways to enrich and deepen their relationship with God.

LESSON SCRIPTURE

2 PETER 1:4–14, KJV

4. Whereby are given unto us exceeding great and precious promises: that by these ye might be partakers of the divine nature, having escaped the corruption that is in the world through lust.

5. And beside this, giving all diligence, add to your faith virtue; and to virtue knowledge;

6. And to knowledge temperance; and to temperance patience; and to patience godliness;

83

7. And to godliness brotherly kindness; and to brotherly kindness charity.

8. For if these things be in you, and abound, they make you that ye shall neither be barren nor unfruitful in the knowledge of our Lord Jesus Christ.

9. But he that lacketh these things is blind, and cannot see afar off, and hath forgotten that he was purged from his old sins.

10. Wherefore the rather, brethren, give diligence to make your calling and election sure: for if ye do these things, ye shall never fall:

11. For so an entrance shall be ministered unto you abundantly into the everlasting king-dom of our Lord and Saviour Jesus Christ.

12. Wherefore I will not be negligent to put you always in remembrance of these things, though ye know them, and be established in the present truth.

13. Yea, I think it meet, as long as I am in this tabernacle, to stir you up by putting you in remembrance;

14. Knowing that shortly I must put off this my tabernacle, even as our Lord Jesus Christ hath shewed me.

BIBLICAL DEFINITIONS

A. **Corruption (2 Peter1:4)** *phthora* (Gk.)—Ruin by moral influences; depravity.
B. **Temperance (v. 6)** *egkrateia* (Gk.)— Holding passions in control.
C. **Brotherly kindness (v.7)** *philadelphia* (Gk.)— Love of people.
D. **Charity (v.7)** *agape* (Gk.)— Godly love.

LIGHT ON THE WORD

Wisdom, Peace, and Grace in Jesus

The Apostle Peter wrote **2 Peter** with a two-fold purpose: not only to warn Christians about the many false teachers who were vying to take them off the foundational truths of the faith, but also to exhort them to grow in the wisdom and knowledge of Jesus Christ—to grow in their faith. At this time, Peter knew that he did not have long to live and therefore, he shared his heart with the Saints. He wanted to warn about what would happen when he was no longer with them and also to remind them that the truth of God's Word is unchanging. As an overseer of the church, called by God, the Apostle Peter took his responsibilities very seriously.

TEACHING THE BIBLE LESSON

LIFE NEED FOR TODAY'S LESSON

AIM: That your students will identify which godly characteristics that Peter lists are active in their lives and which ones need to become activated in their lives.

INTRODUCTION

By the time Peter wrote this second epistle, Paul, his co-laborer in Christ, had probably been martyred, and the church was undergoing fierce persecution. Peter understood that these persecuted believers, to whom he was writing, longed for both knowledge and peace, so he mentions it in his opening salutation to them. He knows also that it is only through their intimate relationship with and personal knowledge of God and of His Son, Jesus Christ, that they might experience the grace and peace they yearned for.

BIBLE LEARNING

AIM: That your students will be empowered to live effective and fruitful lives.

I. PROMISES TO EMPOWER (2 Peter 1:4)

When Peter speaks of promises in this chapter, he means a promise made voluntarily, rather than the result of a request. Here, we see the connection between God's promises and God's grace.

The Promises of God (verse 4)

4. Whereby are given unto us exceeding great and precious promises: that by these ye might be partakers of the divine nature, having escaped the corruption that is in the world through lust.

The Bible is saturated with promises of God. Throughout the Old and New Testaments, there are constant affirmations of the promises made and kept by God. At the dedication of the Temple, King Solomon reminded the people that the period of political peace they were enjoying was a result of God keeping His promises. Solomon declared, "Blessed be the LORD, that hath given rest unto his people Israel, according to all that he promised" (**1 Kings 8:56**).

God's promises are a result of His grace (unmerited favor) and loving-kindness, not because we deserve the blessing. Peter explains that the "exceeding great and precious promises" made to His people are a direct result of the natural goodness of God (**2 Peter 1:4**). Just as it is natural for us to breathe, it is natural for God to bless those He loves. God also desires that His greatest creation be "partakers" or participants in His divine nature and separate from the corrupting forces of the flesh. No doubt Peter's three-year walk with Jesus had made him a personal witness to some of these promises. Peter had learned to appreciate the faithfulness of God through His Word and through personal experience. Present-day Christians can be routinely assured of the promises of God through regular and prayerful study of His Word.

SEARCH THE SCRIPTURES

QUESTION 1

God desires His greatest creation to be _____ of His divine creation.

partakers (participants)

LIGHT ON THE WORD

Promise Keeper

The purpose of God's promises is to enable us to become "partakers of the divine nature." God is at work in us to transform us so we can truly live like those who bear the divine image. God has given us His Word, which enables us to develop new life and godliness. Our Father has made great promises that lead us to a great life. Because He is a great God, He can and will keep all His promises. The Word of God is full of many promises for a range of situations. There are promises for eternal life, forgiveness, healing, joy, peace, and prosperity. God's greatest promise, however, was the gift of His Son, Jesus Christ. Jesus, in turn, promised that God would give the Holy Spirit to us (**John 14:26**).

II. SPIRITUAL GROWTH (2 Peter 1:5–9)

Our union in Christ and our participation in His divinity provide us with the resources we need to live godly lives. This is not to say that we become gods, rather that we are confident we have the living God within us. Peter is careful to note that as Christians, we must give "all diligence" or do our part, too (**verse 5**). We cannot be slack or complacent about our faith walk. We must persevere, and make every effort to perfect our relationship with God.

Spiritual Development is a Process (verses 5–9).

5 And beside this, giving all diligence, add to your faith virtue; and to virtue knowledge; 6 And to knowledge temperance; and to temperance patience; and to patience godliness; 7 And to godliness brotherly kindness; and to brotherly kindness charity. 8 For if these things be in you, and abound, they make you that ye shall neither be barren nor unfruitful in the knowledge of our Lord Jesus Christ. 9 But he that lacketh these things is blind, and cannot see afar off, and hath

forgotten that he was purged from his old sins.

Our spiritual development is an ongoing process, during which there is constant growing, shaping, and refining. The idea of planting flower seeds in a garden and then failing to tend it by watering it and pulling out the weeds is ludicrous! Left unattended, the seeds will dry up and die, or seeds will sprout, but the tiny plants will be overtaken by weeds and strangled. Equally ludicrous is the idea that our faith, left unattended, will grow. Like the neglected flower seeds, the old habits of our former sinful nature will rise like weeds and quickly take hold in our lives.

Our faith is like the seed. Faith is what brings us to Christ in the first place. Now that we have become part of Him, we want our faith to blossom and grow so that we can reflect the very character traits of Jesus. Just as plant seeds need watering, our faith needs nurturing in the Christ-like characteristics that Peter lists in **verses 5–7**: "virtue" (goodness), "knowledge" (understanding), "temperance" (self-control), "patience" (endurance), "godliness" (goodness), "brotherly kindness" (love toward humankind), and "charity" (godly love).

Peter's emphasis on knowledge is especially important because a great portion of this epistle addresses the false teaching that was undermining the church during this period. Peter understood that the only protection the believers had against the false doctrines cropping up was "knowledge," or a firm grasp of the truths of the life, death, and resurrection of Jesus (**verses 3, 5–6**). Equally important is Peter's emphasis on "love" or "charity" (**2 Peter 1:7**). The word used here is godly love. This is the highest form of love and the one expressed by God Himself when He "so loved the world, that he gave his only begotten Son" (**John 3:16**). Love is essential to the growth, maintenance, and work of the Christian community.

QUESTION 2

What is the highest form of love or charity?

Godly love.

LIGHT ON THE WORD
Knowledge and Spiritual Maturity

As we grow spiritually, so too should our knowledge of spiritual truths. The more we know about Jesus, the harder we will strive to understand how to become more like Him. Not only is knowledge critical to Christian maturity and to the development of a godly lifestyle, it is, as Paul claims, our "sword of the Spirit," an integral weapon in spiritual warfare (**Ephesians 6:17**).

III. CONFIDENCE IN OUR CALLING (2 Peter 1:10–11)

Peter admonishes us to be diligent (**verse 10**). While it is true that God must work in us before we can do His will (**Philippians 2:12–23**), it is also true that we must be willing to work for God, and we must cooperate with Him. Instead of following those who are spiritually blind and suffering from forgetfulness, with diligence we are to take our invitation from God and accept the benefits of salvation. Being diligent also means, "being obedient." Living diligently and obediently deepens our awareness of the divine power within us, which gives us all things needed for life and makes our "calling and election sure" (**2 Peter 1:10**).

Diligence and the Everlasting Kingdom (verses 10–11)

10. Wherefore the rather, brethren, give diligence to make your calling and election sure: for if ye do these things, ye shall never fall: 11 For so an entrance shall be ministered unto you abundantly into the everlasting kingdom of our Lord and Saviour Jesus Christ.

Peter now directs his attention to exhorting believers to "give diligence to make your calling and election sure" (**2 Peter 1:10**). Peter is urging the believers to have confidence in their salvation. This confidence is based on living lives that exhibit Christ-like characteristics. It should not be surprising to us that Christians who are not growing in faith will typically lack confidence in their election— their choice of beliefs. It is not enough that we confess Christ. We must grow in Christ in order to have assurance of our salvation.

Peter's reference to "an entrance...ministered unto you abundantly" (**verse 11**) may be a description of the triumphal heavenly welcome that awaits believers who hold the course. Similarly, his reference to the "everlasting kingdom" reminds us that confidence in our calling encourages us to "press toward the mark for the prize of the high calling of God in Christ Jesus" (**Philippians 3:14**). Christians who lack confidence in their calling cannot enjoy the promise of the "prize" of a glorious and eternal life in the presence of God.

QUESTION 3

What does Peter encourage believers to add to knowledge? What does Peter encourage believers to add to patience?

temperance, godliness.

LIGHT ON THE WORD

The Seven Special Qualities

The results of adding the seven qualities mentioned earlier are that they strengthen, encourage, and improve our lives and the lives of those around us. Where these qualities are present, there will be an abundance of good works (**2 Corinthians 9:8**). To "abound" in good works means that we do not just sit around, idle. If these qualities are to exist within us, we must learn to cultivate them so that they produce fruitful results in our lives.

IV. Remember (2 Peter 1:12–14)

Pastors, ministers, and teachers alike are to teach God's precepts. Here, Peter was saying that it was his responsibility to always remind the people of God's goodness toward them. He realized that although they knew the precepts of God, people's tendency to forget may cause them to take things for granted. By reminding them of God's divine grace, mercy, and goodness, Peter was reminding them to never forget the basis for their faith.

Peter's Spiritual Maturity (verses 12–14)

12 Wherefore I will not be negligent to put you always in remembrance of these things, though ye know them, and be established in the present truth. 13 Yea, I think it meet, as long as I am in this tabernacle, to stir you up by putting you in remembrance; 14 Knowing that shortly I must put off this my tabernacle, even as our Lord Jesus Christ hath shewed me.

Peter now turns his attention from teaching and focuses on himself. All that he has said he also has learned for himself. It is not enough that believers learn; we must be willing to share, as Peter does. Peter stresses that he "will not be negligent" in presenting these learned truths to other believers (**2 Peter 1:12**). The apostle is probably about 60 years old when he writes this epistle. He may be recalling the painful time in his life when he was negligent in speaking on behalf of Christ and denied even knowing Jesus. But Peter is not the spiritually immature apostle we first encountered in the Gospels. His priorities have shifted from self to Christ. In this epistle, it is an experienced and spiritually mature man who now emphasizes his solemn duty to witness and who seeks to "stir . . . up" the believers (**verse 13**).

It is clear that Peter is thinking that his death may be imminent when he writes, "shortly I must put off this my tabernacle" (**verse 14**). Some scholars believe Peter may have been imprisoned during the time this letter was written. Although he speaks of his death, he is more concerned that the believers be put "in remembrance" or be reminded of what he has taught them, after he is dead (**verse 15**). Because we know that the young disciple, John Mark, was with Peter (see **1 Peter 5:13**), we may assume that Peter taught him and intended to have John Mark record these teachings. Mark's record is what we now know as the third Gospel or the Gospel of Mark. This particular theory is likely since Mark's Gospel includes facts about Peter that are not mentioned in any of the other Gospels.

QUESTION 4

In **verse 14,** what is Peter saying will come soon?

His death.

LIGHT ON THE WORD
Study the Bible
The Christian who consistently reads the Bible, who knows what he or she believes and why, will rarely be seduced by false teachers, and their phony doctrines. As we become established in the truth, we will not be shaken or moved by the problems we encounter in this world. We can stand on the truth—the Word of God!

BIBLE APPLICATION

AIM: That your students will remember that God perfects us, and it is His desire that we work with Him in developing spiritually.

"I just don't understand you," Isaac complained to his wife. "I told you that I would take care of the utility bill later this week!"

They were arguing, something that seemed to occur more and more frequently these days. It seemed to Isaac that Audrey nitpicked about everything. Some of the bills were behind, but he had assured her that he would make sure they got paid. Why couldn't she just leave it alone?

The bills had been delinquent before, but hadn't he always paid them?

Audrey constantly nagged him about their poor credit rating. Although she hadn't come right out and said it, Isaac felt certain that Audrey blamed him for their not being able to purchase a new car or move out of the apartment and buy a house after eight years. Why didn't she understand that he hadn't had the time to sit down and make a plan to achieve this? Her constant reminders that a bill collector had called or another late notice had come in the mail only seemed to make things worse.

To live godly lives, we must not succumb to laziness; instead, we must take full advantage of the godly resources available to each of us as believers.

STUDENTS' RESPONSES

AIM: That your students will remember to use what God has given to bring glory to Him as well as help one another.

Our spiritual growth in Christ is a constant work in progress. While God perfects us, it is His desire that we work with Him in developing spiritually. Yes, God has provided us with everything that we need, and we should use what He has given us to bring glory to Him as well as help one another. We can only escape the corruption of this world and resist yielding to the flesh and falling back into our old sinful patterns by applying our spiritual power daily. As we go about our routines— conducting business, carrying out parental obligations, enjoying free time, even just running errands— "remembrance" is critical.

PRAYER

Thank You Jesus for taking care of us and providing for us. Guide us in the ways that You want us to go. Remind us that we are to be blessings to others and show love, kindness, and care one to another. In Jesus' name, we pray. Amen.

DIG A LITTLE DEEPER

What happens to human strength if the body gets no exercise? As the old saying goes, "use it or lose it." How does this apply to Christian life? The equipment needed to build physical strength can be as simple as a can of fruit or vegetables or as complicated as the weight training devices at the local gym (https://www.mayoclinic.org/healthy-lifestyle/fitness/in-depth/strength-training/art-20046670).

Scrawny youths with tiny muscles gain strength through exercise: running, jumping, exercising in the gym or even working doing chores at home or on the job. The physical body benefits from exercise, weight training and aerobics, even in old age. "Older people who start to lift weights typically gain muscle mass and strength, as well as better mobility, mental sharpness and metabolic health" (https://www.nytimes.com/2019/03/20/well/move/lifting-weights-exercise-older-aging-muscles-psychology.html). Paul admonishes believers that "physical training is of some value (useful for a little), but godliness (spiritual training) is useful and of value in everything and in every way, for it holds promise for the present life and also for the life which is to come" (1 Timothy 4:8, *Amplified Bible*). To paraphrase: "spiritual exercise, has unlimited value, since it brings blessings for both now and eternity" (*The King James Study Bible*, Thomas Nelson Publishers, 1988, p. 1891). The basic equipment needed to start building spiritual strength is hope provided through faith in our Lord Jesus Christ. Exercising hope, Christians are equipped to build qualities of maturity: virtue, knowledge, self-control, steadfastness, godliness, brotherly affection, and Christian love (2 Peter 1:5-6 *Amplified Bible*).

Therefore, at any stage of life, how can Christians use their equipment – their hope received from God – to avoid developing spiritual atrophy? What practices or exercises build up spiritual strength sufficient to resist sin and false doctrines and to assure eternal life through faith in our Lord and Savior Jesus Christ?

HOW TO SAY IT

Temperance.   TEM-puh-rents.

Diligence.   DIH-luh-jents.

Tabernacle.   TA-buhr-na-kul.

DAILY HOME BIBLE READINGS

MONDAY
Full of Goodness and Knowledge
(Romans 15:14-21)

TUESDAY
The Beginning of Knowledge
(Proverbs 1:2-7)

WEDNESDAY
An Example in Self-Control
(Titus 1:5-9)

THURSDAY
Enduring to the End
(Matthew 24:9-14)

FRIDAY
A Life of Godliness and Dignity
(1 Timothy 2:1-7)

SATURDAY
Love for One Another
(1 Peter 3:8-12)

SUNDAY
Standing on God's Precious Promises
(2 Peter 1:4-14)

PREPARE FOR NEXT SUNDAY

Read **1 Peter 4:1-11** and study "Hope through Stewardship."

Sources:

Merriam-Webster Online Dictionary. http://www. merriam-webster.com (accessed November 3, 2011).

New Testament Greek Lexicon. http://www. biblestudytools.com/lexicons/greek (accessed October 31, 2011).

Packer, J. I. and M. C. Tenney, eds. Illustrated Manners and Customs of the Bible.

Nashville, TN: Thomas Nelson, 1980. 41, 537-538, 551.

Zodhiates, Spiros. Complete Word Study Dictionary: New Testament. Iowa Falls, IA: World Bible Publish- ers, 1992.

COMMENTS / NOTES:

HOPE THROUGH STEWARDSHIP

BIBLE BASIS: 1 Peter 4:1–11

BIBLE TRUTH: Jesus provides the example that we are to serve one another.

MEMORY VERSE: "As every man hath received the gift, even so minister the same one to another, as good stewards of the manifold grace of God" (1 Peter 4:10, KJV).

LESSON AIM: By the end of the lesson, we will: KNOW the cost of discipleship; FEEL able to recall a time when we relied on God's power; and LOOK for opportunities to serve others.

BACKGROUND SCRIPTURES: 1 Peter 4, KJV — Read and incorporate the insights gained from the Background Scriptures into your study of the lesson.

TEACHER PREPARATION

MATERIALS NEEDED: Bibles, (several different versions), Quarterly Commentary/Teacher Manual, Adult Quarterly, teaching resources such as charts, worksheets/handouts, paper, pens, and pencils.

OTHER MATERIALS NEEDED / TEACHER'S NOTES:

_____

_____

LESSON OVERVIEW

LIFE NEED FOR TODAY'S LESSON

That your students will know that following Jesus is not always comfortable or easy.

BIBLE APPLICATION

To better understand the expectations that come with following Christ.

BIBLE LEARNING

To understand the physical sufferings Jesus endured for us.

STUDENTS' RESPONSES

Students will decide ways to serve others that exemplify the character of Christ.

LESSON SCRIPTURE

1 PETER 4:1–11, KJV

1. Forasmuch then as Christ hath suffered for us in the flesh, arm yourselves likewise with the same mind: for he that hath suffered in the flesh hath ceased from sin;

2. That he no longer should live the rest of his time in the flesh to the lusts of men, but to the will of God.

3. For the time past of our life may suffice us to have wrought the will of the Gentiles, when we walked in lasciviousness, lusts, ex- cess of wine, revellings, banquetings, and abominable idolatries:

4. Wherein they think it strange that ye run not with them to the same excess of riot, speaking evil of you:

5. Who shall give account to him that is ready to judge the quick and the dead.

6. For for this cause was the gospel preached also to them that are dead, that they might be judged according to men in the flesh, but live according to God in the spirit.

7. But the end of all things is at hand: be ye therefore sober, and watch unto prayer.

8. And above all things have fervent charity among yourselves: for charity shall cover the multitude of sins.

9. Use hospitality one to another without grudging.

1o. As every man hath received the gift, even so minister the same one to another, as good stewards of the manifold grace of God.

11. If any man speak, let him speak as the oracles of God; if any man minister, let him do it as of the ability which God giveth: that God in all things may be glorified through Jesus Christ, to whom be praise and dominion for ever and ever. Amen.

BIBLICAL DEFINITIONS

A. Flesh (1 Peter 4:1) *sarx* (Gk.)—Used to denote the body (as opposed to the soul or spirit), or as the symbol of what is external; a human being.
B. Lasciviousness (v. 3) *aselgeia* (Gk.)— Depravity, iniquity, wickedness.

LIGHT ON THE WORD

"And when the day of Pentecost was fully come, they were all with one accord in one place. And they were all filled with the Holy Ghost, and began to speak with other tongues as the Spirit gave them utterance" (**Acts 2:1, 4**). Men from every nation on earth were in Jerusalem that day and were amazed when they heard these unlearned men speaking in their own languages. This same Peter stood and preached a 3,000 souls-saving message, and many were added to the church that day.

TEACHING THE BIBLE LESSON

LIFE NEED FOR TODAY'S LESSON

AIM: That your students will be willing to follow the example of Christ.

INTRODUCTION
The Day of Pentecost
Fifty days after the Passover Lamb had been slain, there were 120 of Christ's disciples gathered in an upper room per their Master's instructions, waiting on power from on high. Secluded in this room in Jerusalem, Peter, the author of our Scripture text, initiated the selection process for replacing Judas who had betrayed Christ. Among the requirements to be a replacement were: **1)** having been with Jesus from the time of John's baptism; **2)** to be a witness of Jesus' resurrection; and **3)** having beheld His ascension into Heaven. The two men selected had been faithful followers and met these conditions. Of the two, Matthias was selected to complete the number of the 12 apostles.

BIBLE LEARNING

AIM: That your students will discipline themselves to stay away from evil and follow the ways of Christ.

I. CHRIST'S EXAMPLE (1 Peter 4:1–2)

"Forasmuch then as Christ hath suffered for us in the flesh, arm yourselves likewise with the same mind: for he that hath suffered in the flesh hath ceased from sin" (**1 Peter 4:1**). Were Peter alive today, he may have worded this verse something like this: "Followers of Christ must put on the mind of Christ in order not to fulfill the lusts of the flesh. This is not Burger King˚; you cannot have it your way." Peter knew that flesh is an enemy of the Spirit. In order to maintain the mind of Christ, we must cut off the old fleshly habits and desires. We must renew our minds on a daily basis.

The Suffering of Jesus (verses 1–2)

1 Forasmuch then as Christ hath suffered for us in the flesh, arm yourselves likewise with the same mind: for he that hath suffered in the flesh hath ceased from sin; 2 That he no longer should live the rest of his time in the flesh to the lusts of men, but to the will of God.

Peter talked in chapter three about Christ's suffering and refers to it in this section. Christ's suffering occurred in His body while on the Cross and includes emotional suffering as well as physical. Peter asks his readers in Asia Minor to "arm" themselves with the same attitude as Christ. Therefore, one should equip themselves for a battle or "take on the same mind." Sinfulness is too serious to be neglected. There should be no compromise with sin because it brings spiritual death. When one faces a deadly enemy, one has to take every necessary action to subdue and overcome this enemy. **Hebrews 12:4** suggests that the struggle against sin may even require the shedding of blood or specific physical actions.

In **1 Peter 4:1**, the statement "he who has suffered in his body is done with sin" may seem difficult to understand. The word for "body" is generally translated "flesh," and is understood to refer to the sinful nature in us. It is not to say that suffering can remove sin in one's life, but rather as one commentary stated: "If anyone suffers for doing good and still faithfully obeys [God] in spite of suffering, that person has made a clean break with sin" (*Life Application Bible*, 2263). **Galatians 5:16–22** talks about life in the flesh and life in the Spirit, and there Paul entreats his readers to walk according to the Spirit because life in the Spirit is opposed to life in the flesh.

In **1 Corinthians 9:27,** Paul says that his strategy to avoid falling into sin is to "bring (his body) into subjection." He then illustrated Israel's failure in the desert due to immorality and idolatry.

It is obvious that these passages are not suggesting a kind of salvation by works or atonement of sins by any other means. The only lesson drawn from them is the responsibility of the believer in disciplining his life to shun evil. These disciplines can be painful sometimes.

SEARCH THE SCRIPTURES

QUESTION 1

Peter talks about the suffering of Christ. What type of suffering is he referring to?

Physical suffering.

LIGHT ON THE WORD

The Attitude of Suffering

The attitude of suffering for a life of holiness is a Christian's lifetime resolution, a determination to live in sanctification. This means that a believer will not satisfy the cravings of fleshly desire. In **Galatians 5:20–21**, we find the list of these evil human desires. This resolution is an outcome of willingness to suffer bodily struggles—physical and emotional— as mentioned in the passage from **1 Peter 4**. The subjection of the body is a prerequisite to a life of sanctification.

The person who resolutely turns from gratifying evil human desires orients his or her life toward fulfilling what is pleasing to God. Paul stresses that the will of God is a life of holiness. The resolution to fulfill the will of God will keep us away from evil human desires. The reason is that the will of God and the cravings of our heart are in opposition. We will either obey God's will or follow our own inclinations, not both at the same time.

II. CHRIST'S TEACHINGS: PUT OFF THE OLD, PUT ON THE NEW (1 Peter 4:3–6)

Think back to the time when you first got saved. In order to be an excellent witness of that precious gift of salvation, old friends had to go. Even though they may have ridiculed and talked about you, to be a positive witness for God, you had to suffer that separation from the old lifestyle. The Bible tells us that evil communications corrupt good manners (**1 Corinthians 15:33**). A choice had to be made; you had to tell yourself, "Either I'll continue in my old sinful ways, or I will change the company I keep and walk in my salvation—be sanctified and filled with the Holy Ghost."

The Response to Change (verses 3–6)
3 For the time past of our life may suffice us to have wrought the will of the Gentiles, when we walked in lasciviousness, lusts, excess of wine, revellings, banquetings, and abominable idolatries: 4 Wherein they think it strange that ye run not with them to the same excess of riot, speaking evil of you: 5 Who shall give account to him that is ready to judge the quick and the dead. 6 For this cause was the gospel preached also to them that are dead, that they might be judged according to men in the flesh, but live according to God in the spirit.

The sins described here refer to idol worship. Some cultic practices and immorality were combined. This is not a new thing. The Israelites were enticed by the Moabites to sin through their cultic practices (**Numbers 25:1–3; Revelation 2:14**). Baal worship and many other pagans' worship included immoral practices. These orgies are still around today in occult circles but also in modern forms of entertainment. So in this letter, Peter mentions these vices and also names the context in which the vices take place. Not only should a Christian shun these sins, but the context in which these sins happen should be avoided, too.

The Christians whom Peter is addressing in the letter were part of a culture, and therefore many were involved in whatever was practiced in that culture. When they received Christ, many refrained from indulging in the reproachable practices of their former lifestyle. Their refusal to conform to their society's corrupt way of life was noticed by their former friends and present neighbors and colleagues. These people could not understand how those who had followed them in a life of dissipation could now withdraw themselves.

Their abstention from idolatry and immoral behavior brought the fury of their former mates. In the early church, because Christians refused to take part in the worship of the king, they were portrayed as enemies of the state. It was certainly painful to bear wrongful abuse, knowing the innocence of your behavior and the righteousness of your choices. This is why Peter advised his readers to have a clear conscience and a good conduct which would confuse those who spoke maliciously about them (**3:16**).

The detractors of the Christians in Asia Minor will not go unpunished. They will have to give an account to God for their false accusations and their slander. God is the Judge of humankind. Those who are still alive and those who are already dead will all be judged. This judgment is a prospect of the final judgment.

The judgment of God is done in righteousness and fairness. The statement here could mean that those who are now dead heard about the Gospel during their lifetime. In this way their judgment is based on their response to the Gospel while they were alive.

Being "judged according to men in the flesh" most-likely refers to physical death, but life "according to God in the spirit" refers to the judgment that decides the eternal fate of one's soul.

QUESTION 2

How will people respond when Christians turn from their evil and wicked ways?

They will think it is strange that you are not doing what you used to do.

LIGHT ON THE WORD

Peter writes for us to be conscious of the judgment of Christ. It has often been said that we must not fear someone who has neither heaven nor hell to put us in. In other words, man can only do so much to you. Jesus Christ alone has the power to judge. The Gospel has the power to turn lives around that are on a collision course with death, damnation, and destruction. Praise God for the power in the blood of Jesus. As servants of humankind, we must preach this great Gospel for all to hear.

III. GOD'S TEACHINGS: BE SOBER, WATCHFUL, AND PRAYERFUL (1 Peter 4:7–9)

As one vintage song of the church proclaims, "In times like these, we need an anchor." We are admonished to pray without ceasing (**1 Thessalonians 5:17**). Jesus explained to His disciples, when asked about the end times, that there would be many signs. Among them are: deceivers of many, nations rising against nations, wars and rumors of wars, famine, pestilence, and earthquakes in many different places (**Matthew 24:3–7**).

This, however, is only the beginning of the end. Peter admonishes the faithful to be sober and watchful in prayer. One preacher puts it like this: "Pray with one eye open!"

Judgment Day is Coming (verses 7–9)
7 But the end of all things is at hand: be ye therefore sober, and watch unto prayer. 8 And above all things have fervent charity among yourselves: for charity shall cover the multitude of sins. 9 Use hospitality one to another without grudging.

The "end of all things" reminds us of the final judgment. Peter wants his readers to be alert—because the end "is at hand"—and to focus in anticipation of the end of the world. The judgment day is getting nearer, and there is a need for Christians to pray.

The Christian community needs to express love among its members. Love "shall cover a multitude of sins" is a citation of **Proverbs 10:12**. It means that when there is love ("charity" as **1 Peter 4:8** states), the brethren will forgive and overlook the sins of others; however, that does not imply complacency, either. We should strive to live out the second greatest commandment: to love our neighbors as ourselves (**Matthew 22:39**).

As Christians, the blood of Jesus has covered our sins. God did not hold us accountable for our sins, but He forgave us in Christ. In turn, we have to forgive each other and build unity (**Colossians 3:13**).

Love was also expressed in offering hospitality to fellow Christians as they traveled, particularly since in that era hotel-type accommodations were extremely rare. This hospitality consisted of providing shelter and food, especially to those who were traveling from place to place, doing the work of God.

However, a host's patience can really be tried by a guest's personality. In any circumstances, Peter urges the recipients of his letter to exercise hospitality "without grumbling" (**1 Peter 4:9 NIV**). As human beings, sometimes we abuse privileges such as hospitality, and this can create difficulties in relationships. It is recorded that by A.D. 100, in Asia, guidelines had been adopted to prevent abuses. Peter Davids points out such an example, in which a guest could not stay more than three days at the expense of the host (**First Epistle of Peter**, 159).

The theme of hospitality was so important that, in New Testament times, it was part of the qualification for elders in the church and for enrolled widows, as noted by David (**First Epistle of Peter**, 159).

LIGHT ON THE WORD
It's All About Love
We can all tell when another person loves us. Even little children know when they are loved. We are to love each other with a fervent love. It has been said that love is an action word. Just think how much better it is to add energy and authenticity to the love that we share with our fellow Christians. According to Peter, this love will cover a multitude of sins. Now, it may be said that there are no skeletons in your cupboard, but grace is sufficient for all. Use love to cover another's faults; you may need that same favor returned to you someday.

IV. GOD'S TEACHINGS: GIFTS OF HONOR (1 Peter 4:10–11)

10 As every man hath received the gift, even so minister the same one to another, as good stewards of the manifold grace of God. 11 If any man speak, let him speak as the oracles of God; if any man minister, let him do it as of the ability which God giveth: that God in all things may be glorified through Jesus Christ, to whom be praise and dominion for ever and ever. Amen.

So often we think of stewardship as related to money or things of material value. Here, Peter applies stewardship to the manifold grace of God. Let's examine that concept further. Earlier, in **1 Peter 1**, we were given the concept that our faith, through trial, is more precious than gold. Jesus tells us, "Seek ye first the kingdom of God and his righteousness; and all these things shall be added unto you" (**Matthew 6:33**). As we seek God's kingdom with the mind of Christ, everything else tends to fall into place. We must seek God's kingdom and His righteousness.

Gifts are given according to God's grace. These godly gifts are to be used to glorify Him and Him alone.

God's Gifts (verses 10–11)
One of the problems of walking in the flesh is that flesh has a desire to be glorified. When we take on our new nature in Christ, that attitude won't work. As the saying goes, "oil and water don't mix." The same theory applies to this subject: God's gifts and our flesh don't mix. We are accountable to God and our fellow persons to be ministers of righteousness, upholding the integrity of our calling in Christ Jesus.

QUESTION 4
Who is to be glorified with the gifts that we have received and are to share with others?

God through Jesus Christ.

LIGHT ON THE WORD
Naturally, Bible scholars see the similarity and cohesiveness of this passage of Scripture and Apostle Paul's message to the church at Corinth in **1 Corinthians 12** and other passages. The bottom line is, I need you and you need me. We are all fellow servants of our King. It is tantamount that Jesus Christ receives all the

praise and glory from the service that we render to Him and one another.

In the words of Jesus Christ Himself, we are made to know that "he that is greatest among you shall be your servant" (**Matthew 23:11**). Let us go forth, empowered to serve.

BIBLE APPLICATION

AIM: That your students believe and know that they have the power of the Holy Ghost in their spirit to witness to people in their community and in the world.

STUDENTS' RESPONSES

AIM: That your students will share God's love to bring transformation to God's people.

The American culture is one of me first, self-reliance, and downright selfishness. Contrast how as servants of the Most High God we can be a countercultural force in the world today. Knowing up front that this will not be an easy road to walk, we must identify ways that we can minister to each other in order to encourage steadfastness in accomplishing the goal of impacting the world around us.

PRAYER

Dear Heavenly Father, words cannot express the deep love and appreciation that we have for You allowing Your Son Jesus to die on the Cross and rise from the dead for all of us. Your love, grace, and mercy extend far more than we can imagine. We celebrate and honor You for Your tender kindness and keeping us even when we sin and forget about You. Thank You, Thank You, and Thank You. In Jesus' name, we pray. Amen.

DIG A LITTLE DEEPER

Evoking the image of a steward, Peter urges Christians to take care of themselves and one another by being "good stewards." In the original text, the word translated from Greek to English as steward is *oikonomos* (*oikos* – house; and *nemo* – to arrange), literally meaning the manager of a household or an estate: usually a slave or a freeman [one who had been a slave] (*Vine's Expository Dictionary of New Testament Words*, 1952, p. 74). Webster's Dictionary adds these modern examples: "an employee on a ship, airplane, bus, or train who manages the provisioning of food and attends passengers."

Modern travelers might associate the word, steward or stewardess, with those responsible for their comfort and safety on airplanes. Recently, many of them have been verbally or physically abused by angry passengers. Likewise, waiters and waitresses in restaurants report an uptick in mistreatment from patrons impatient with slower service resulting from more people leaving service occupations. While these "stewards" may also be leaving their jobs because they are underpaid, what about the stewards Peter addresses in his letter? How can Christian stewards expect to be treated? What will be their reward?

Jesus described what it means to be one of God's good stewards and how good and bad stewards would be rewarded when He returns. He said the "faithful and wise steward" would be richly blessed but the steward (servant) who abused other servants and began "to eat and drink, and to be drunken" would be "cut asunder" and would receive "his portion with the unbelievers" (Luke 12:41-46). Peter heard Jesus' warning and passed it on to the believers who read his letter. Peter addressed their stewardship of two houses: their own bodies and the body of Christ. Paul warned that the sin described in 1 Peter 4: 3 "defiles" the physical body and/or the church, "the temple of God" and the "temple of the Holy Ghost" (1 Corinthians 3:16-17 and 6:19 and 2 Corinthians 6:16-17). Peter advised that when good stewards of their bodies turn away from sin, they could expect abuse from their former associates. Should Christians who are serving other believers also expect abuse? And if so, how should they respond?

HOW TO SAY IT

Lasciviousness.   l u h - S I V - e e - u h s - n u h s.
Pentecost.   PEHN-tee-kawst.

DAILY HOME BIBLE READINGS

MONDAY
Trust God to Provide
(Luke 12:22–28)

TUESDAY
The Unfailing Treasure
(Luke 12:29–34)

WEDNESDAY
Be Alert and Ready
(Luke 12:35–40)

THURSDAY
The Faithful and Prudent Manager
(Luke 12:41–48)

FRIDAY
The Perfect Gift from Above
(James 1:12–18)

SATURDAY
Faithful in Little and Much
(Luke 16:10–13)

SUNDAY
Good Stewards of God's Grace
(1 Peter)

PREPARE FOR NEXT SUNDAY

Read **2 Peter 3:1–15a**, and read "Hope in the Day of the Lord."

COMMENTS / NOTES:

HOPE IN THE DAY OF THE LORD

BIBLE BASIS: 2 Peter 3:1–15a

BIBLE TRUTH: The writer of 2 Peter urges his readers to be patient and live holy, godly lives.

MEMORY VERSE: "The Lord is not slack concerning his promise, as some men count slackness; but is longsuffering to us-ward, not willing that any should perish, but that all should come to repentance" (2 Peter 3:9, KJV).

LESSON AIM: By the end of the lesson, we will: UNDERSTAND the significance of holy living; FEEL CONFIDENT that Christ will return for His church; and ANTICIPATE the day when God will make all things new.

BACKGROUND SCRIPTURES: 2 Peter 3, KJV — Read and incorporate the insights gained from the Background Scriptures into your study of the lesson.

TEACHER PREPARATION

MATERIALS NEEDED: Bibles, (several different versions), Quarterly Commentary/Teacher Manual, Adult Quarterly, teaching resources such as charts, worksheets/handouts, paper, pens, and pencils.

OTHER MATERIALS NEEDED / TEACHER'S NOTES:

_____

_____

LESSON OVERVIEW

LIFE NEED FOR TODAY'S LESSON

That students will appreciate that God calls us to live lives that are pleasing to Him.

BIBLE LEARNING

To develop why God wants us, His people, to be ready and waiting for Christ to return.

BIBLE APPLICATION

To understand the significance of holy living and feel confident that Christ will return for His church.

STUDENTS' RESPONSES

Students will think of ways to serve others that exemplify the character of Christ.

LESSON SCRIPTURE

PETER 3:1–15a, KJV

3:1. This second epistle, beloved, I now write unto you; in both which I stir up your pure minds by way of remembrance:

2. That ye may be mindful of the words which were spoken before by the holy prophets, and of the commandment of us the apostles of the Lord and Saviour:

3. Knowing this first, that there shall come in the last days scoffers, walking after their own lusts,

4. And saying, Where is the promise of his coming? for since the fathers fell asleep, all things continue as they were from the beginning of the creation.

5. For this they willingly are ignorant of, that by the word of God the heavens were of old, and the earth standing out of the water and in the water:

6. Whereby the world that then was, being overflowed with water, perished:

7. But the heavens and the earth, which are now, by the same word are kept in store, reserved unto fire against the day of judgment and perdition of ungodly men.

8. But, beloved, be not ignorant of this one thing, that one day is with the Lord as a thousand years, and a thousand years as one day.

9. The Lord is not slack concerning his promise, as some men count slackness; but is longsuffering to us-ward, not willing that any should perish, but that all should come to repentance.

10. But the day of the Lord will come as a thief in the night; in the which the heavens shall pass away with a great noise, and the elements shall melt with fervent heat, the earth also and the works that are therein shall be burned up.

11. Seeing then that all these things shall be dissolved, what manner of persons ought ye to be in all holy conversation and godliness,

12. Looking for and hasting unto the coming of the day of God, wherein the heavens being on fire shall be dissolved, and the elements shall melt with fervent heat?

13. Nevertheless we, according to his promise, look for new heavens and a new earth, wherein dwelleth righteousness.

14. Wherefore, beloved, seeing that ye look for such things, be diligent that ye may be found of him in peace, without spot, and blameless.

15. And account that the longsuffering of our Lord is salvation;

BIBLICAL DEFINITIONS

A. Epistle (2 Peter 3:1) *epistole* (Gk.)—A letter, correspondence.
B. Scoffers (v. 3) *empaiktes* (Gk.) Mockers; denotes non-believers.

LIGHT ON THE WORD

The phrase the "Day of the Lord" presents different meanings. Theologians interpret this various ways, but it certainly is the time when Jesus returns, whether in judgment for unbelievers or with everlasting joy for the followers of Christ. Instead of fearing or focusing on the time or day when Jesus returns, Christians in particular should do God's will until Jesus comes back. The day Jesus returns will be a day of rejoicing for those who will be with Jesus forever.

TEACHING THE BIBLE LESSON

LIFE NEED FOR TODAY'S LESSON

AIM: That your students will know that Peter wants believers to live life knowing and anticipating Jesus' return.

INTRODUCTION

Peter Challenges False Teachers

The Apostle Peter wrote this text not only to warn Christians about false teachers, but also to exhort them to grow in their faith and in the knowledge of their Lord and Savior, Jesus Christ. One principle area of attack from false teachers was the return and future judgment of Christ. If there was no future judgment, then people were free to live as they chose. In the final chapter of his second epistle, Peter directly challenges this error.

BIBLE LEARNING

AIM: That your students will discipline themselves to trust God's Word.

I. BELIEVE GOD'S WORD
(2 Peter 3:1–4)

The last days (end times) started with the first coming of Jesus (**Hebrews 1:2**), which initiated all of the events that had to happen in order for the end to come. The Greek text for **2 Peter 3:3** reads literally "scoffing scoffers will come." The repetition of the word is a way of adding emphasis. A "scoffer" is someone who ridicules, mocks, or makes fun of others.

"Lusts" in this context is "strong desires for something forbidden." "Walking after" is also translated as "walking according to." These scoffers discard God's revelation of the correct path through His Word and instead chart a path for themselves based on their desires.

Stir It Up (verses 1–4)
1 This second epistle, beloved, I now write unto you; in both which I stir up your pure minds by way of remembrance: 2 That ye may be mindful of the words which were spoken before by the holy prophets, and of the commandment of us the apostles of the Lord and Saviour: 3 Knowing this first, that there shall come in the last days scoffers, walking after their own lusts, 4 And saying, Where is the promise of his coming? for since the fathers fell asleep, all things continue as they were from the beginning of the creation.

Peter intended to "stir up" the people's memory (**2 Peter 3:1**). To "stir up" means "to fully awaken." The apostle suggests three areas where the people's memory needed awakening: the words of the holy prophets, the commandments

of the apostles, and the commandments of Christ.

Peter realized that in these "last days" many people would question Christian beliefs in the Lord (**3:3**). These people would cause others to have doubts about the authority of God's Word. Peter called these unbelievers "scoffers" (**verse 3**). "Scoffers" are false teachers who mock the truth. The apostle had already warned the people that these scoffers would infiltrate the church with their "damnable heresies" (**2:1**). Some even went as far as denying the deity of Christ.

The "last days" refer to the period between the first and second coming of Christ. During this period, ungodly teachers will deny that Christ is coming back to execute judgment. The false teachers say, "Where is the promise of his coming? for since the fathers fell asleep, all things continue as they were from the beginning of the creation" (**3:4**).

It is sad that people are deceived into believing Christ is not coming again. However, Peter's message is clear: Do not listen to these scoffers and do not follow them. God's Word is true and His promises are unfailing.

SEARCH THE SCRIPTURES

QUESTION 1

What are the three areas that the Apostle Peter suggests where the people's memory needed awakening?

1) the words of the holy prophets;

2) the commandments of the apostles; and

3) the commandments of the apostles of the Lord and Saviour.

LIGHT ON THE WORD

The Questioning Scoffers
"Where is the promise of his coming?" is a literal translation of the Greek; it may also be translated "Where is His promised coming?" The word

"coming" may also be translated "appearing," and is used frequently in the New Testament to refer to Christ's return (cf. **Matthew 24:27; 1 Thessalonians 4:15**).

The argument advanced by these scoffers is that "all things continue as they were"— nothing has changed "since the fathers fell asleep" (**2 Peter 3:4**). The "fathers" are probably the Old Testament patriarchs. To the scoffers, the thought of the world as we know it ending is laughable.

II. BELIEVE IN GOD'S CREATION (2 Peter 3:5–9)

Since the scoffers refer to the earth's beginning, Peter's response to their argument also goes back to the beginning. He accuses them of being "willingly... ignorant." The Greek text here is difficult to translate, but a word-for-word rendering reads something like "it escapes them willingly." The scoffers, then, deliberately fail to note that before the days of creation, the world was covered with water (**Genesis 1:2**). The land on which we live came out of water by God's Word alone (**1:9**).

The world, then, "overflowed with water" and "perished" (**2 Peter 3:6**). This is a clear reference to Noah's time, in which the world flooded within forty days. Peter's point here is this: It took only God's Word to create the earth, and it took only another Word from Him for that same earth to be destroyed.

Intentionally Ignoring God's Creation (verses 5–9)

5 For this they willingly are ignorant of, that by the word of God the heavens were of old, and the earth standing out of the water and in the water: 6 Whereby the world that then was, being overflowed with water, perished: 7 But the heavens and the earth, which are now, by the same word are kept in store, reserved unto fire against the day of judgment and perdition of ungodly men. 8 But, beloved, be not ignorant of this one thing, that one day is with the Lord as a thousand years, and a thousand years as one day. 9 The Lord is not slack concerning his promise, as some men count slackness; but is long-suffering to us-ward, not willing that any should perish, but that all should come to repentance.

The scoffers do not believe the truth of God's Word. They portray God's truth as a moral fable. These false teachers purposely forget that God created the heavens and the earth. To refute their heresy, Peter reminds his readers of God's creative power. First, he reminds them of how God, by His Word, rolled back the waters to create dry land (**verse 5; Genesis 1:9–10**). God used the same waters that He rolled back to destroy the old world in the days of Noah and his family (**2 Peter 3:6**). He did not spare the old world when His people disobeyed Him (**2:5**), and He will not spare the current world. God has already decided the world's fate and declared it through Christ and His apostles.

Scoffers need to be warned that God's Word is true. They think He has forgotten His creation, so they feel that they can live any way they choose. They fail to realize that God is being patient with us. Scoffers fail to understand that because His desire is to save and not destroy, God does not measure time according to human standards. God is so gracious, and Peter reminds his readers of this as he writes, "that one day is with the Lord as a thousand years, and a thousand years as one day" (**3:8**). God can accomplish in one day what might take a thousand years, and He may take a thousand years to accomplish what might seem to be a one-day task.

"Kept in store" means "gathered up, stored up." The Greek text makes it clear that "fire" is the reason it has been stored. Peter will expand on this concept in **verse 10**.

"Against" here means "for" or "unto." The burning by fire will not occur until the Day of Judgment. On that day, Christ will judge all people dead and living (**1 Peter 4:5**). Christians can face that day with confidence because judgment will mean vindication for the righteous (**1 John 4:17**)—and Christians, by faith, have the righteousness of Christ applied to their account (**Romans 4:24**). But Peter here focuses on the fate of the wicked. In **2 Peter 3:7**, "perdition" means "destruction, annihilation, ruin." "Ungodly" means "impious, destitute of reverential awe toward God." The ungodly will receive the full measure of God's righteous wrath for their failure to honor Him as God (**Romans 2:5**). We have God's Word on this truth.

"Be not ignorant" is the same Greek word as in the phrase "willingly . . . ignorant" in **verse 5**. Peter instructs Christians to not make the same mistake as unbelievers who choose to neglect God's truth.

Peter alludes to **Psalm 90:4**: "a thousand years in thy sight are but as yesterday." The Scriptures teach that God is eternal (**Deuteronomy 33:27; Job 36:26; Isaiah 40:28**)—having no beginning and no end (**Psalm 90:2; 1 John 2:13; Revelation 1:4**). The brevity of our lifespan colors our concept of time. The Scriptures compare the human lifespan to dust and grass, which blows away and withers (**Psalm 103:14–16; Isaiah 40:6–7**).

QUESTION 2

Compare our measurement of one day to the Lord's measurement of one day.

"that one day is with the Lord as a thousand years, and a thousand years as one day."

LIGHT ON THE WORD

God's Not the Problem

The problem is not with God, but with some people's finite, foolish perception. They forget that God is infinitely greater than they are. In their delusion, they conclude that God is too slow.

Peter goes on to reveal that the reason Jesus has not yet returned is because God is "longsuffering" which means "to bear up under provocation without complaining, be patient." Ironically, those who accuse God of being late are themselves proving His patience. A harsh, vindictive god would soon lose patience with such insolence, but the God of heaven and earth does not change His mind, and He continues according to His plan. His delay, if we must call it that, is for the sake of those He came to save. God's desire is that none should "perish" here means "to be ruined or lost"—a reference to eternal, spiritual death. The Scriptures repeatedly reveal God's kindness toward the lost and His concern even for those who are His enemies.

"Come to repentance" (**2 Peter 3:9**) is the alternative to perishing—repentance, therefore, is the way to life. "Repentance" is "a change of mind, a turning around." The message of the Gospel is that all sinful people must repent—turn from their sin to God (**Acts 26:20**)—and put their full faith in Jesus to save them (**Romans 10:9**).

III. BELIEVE IN GOD'S PROMISE (2 Peter 3:10–13)

Peter emphatically declares, "The day of the Lord will come as a thief in the night" (**verse 10**). According to Spiros Zodhiates—a Greek American Bible scholar and author— the "day of the Lord" represents the second coming of Christ and the occasion when God will actively intervene to punish sin. The term also refers to the time immediately before the creation of the new heaven and earth (*Complete Word Study Dictionary: New Testament,* 710).

All Things Shall Dissolve Away
(verses 10–13)

10 But the day of the Lord will come as a thief in the night; in the which the heavens shall pass away with a great noise, and the elements shall melt with fervent heat, the earth also and the works that are therein shall be burned up. 11 Seeing then that all these things shall be dissolved, what manner of persons ought ye to be in all holy conversation and godliness, 12 Looking for and hasting unto the coming of the day of God, wherein the heavens being on fire shall be dissolved, and the elements shall melt with fervent heat? 13 Nevertheless we, according to his promise, look for new heavens and a new earth, wherein dwelleth righteousness.

The "Day of the Lord" is one of the Bible's many ways of referring to the day of Christ's second coming. It is also referred to as "the Day of Judgment" or simply "the Day." In the Old Testament, the "Day of the Lord" is portrayed as a day of wrath and destruction for the wicked and the enemies of Israel (**Joel 1:15; Isaiah 13:6, 9**). The New Testament also speaks of judgment on that day (**Romans 2:5**), and emphasizes that it will be a day of vindication, deliverance, and victory for the people of God (**1 Corinthians 1:8; Philippians 1:6; 1 Thessalonians 5:9**).

Peter describes an unprecedented devastation that will happen on the "Day of the Lord." He lists three kinds of devastation: the heavens passing away with a great noise, the elements melting, and the earth burning up (along with the works thereon). Other passages in both the Old and New Testaments refer to the "passing away" of the created universe (cf. **Matthew 24:35; Revelation 21:1**), but Peter's account here is perhaps the most vivid in all of Scripture.

In **2 Peter 3:10**, the Greek verb phrase that describes "the elements shall melt with fervent heat" could be translated literally as "the elements being burned up will be dissolved." The "elements" could refer to either the material building blocks of the physical universe or the heavenly bodies.

The best, most accurate Greek manuscripts do not contain the verb "burned up;" instead, we find words that mean "find out, discover." The most likely meaning of the final phrase of this verse is that the earth and everything done in it will be exposed and laid bare, after which God will transform the creation—a new heavens and earth.

In **verse 12**, the verb "dissolved" is the same word used in **verse 10** to describe the melting of the elements. It means "to aloose, release, abolish, or destroy." "All these things" means literally "everything." Christians are to live in the awareness that everything we own or accumulate will someday pass away. The only things that will have eternal value are the things we did to serve the Lord (cf. **1 Corinthians 3:13–15**). Furthermore, the "Day of the Lord" also means the revelation of all that has been done—good or evil (see comments on **2 Peter 3:10**).

"Hasting" means "to desire earnestly, to cause something to happen or come into being by exercising special effort." Jesus taught us that we can hasten His coming by praying for the coming of His kingdom (**Matthew 6:10**) and by spreading the Gospel to all peoples (**24:14**).

Verse 13 presents the new heaven and new earth (promised in **Isaiah 65:17**) that will be perfect because all traces and effects of sin will be completely wiped out. Satan and his demons will be thrown into hell and no unrighteous person will gain admittance to the new heaven and new earth (**1 Corinthians 6:9–10; Revelation 21:8**).

In **2 Peter 3:13**, "dwelleth" means "reside, inhabit." It denotes permanent residency. This world as we know it (under God's curse and the contaminating impact of sin) is only our temporary home; the new heaven and new earth are the permanent home for the righteous.

The word "new" is used in the New Testament to refer to newness that contrasts with the obsolete—the New Covenant, for example. Peter's choice of new is consistent with the message of the rest of the Scriptures: the new heaven and new earth will be a renewal, not a replacement, of God's good creation.

QUESTION 3

What things will be dissolved?

All things.

LIGHT ON THE WORD

New Heaven and New Earth

Peter says that on this day, "the heavens shall pass away with a great noise" (**verse 10**). The Greek word translated "great noise" means "with a great crash." The apostle declares the earth will be dissolved, and not only the earth, but all the "works that are therein." Everything that humanity has ever created, invented, or built will be utterly consumed.

IV. BE AT PEACE WITH HIM
(2 Peter 3:14–15a)

Peter uses the word for "look" once each in **verses 12**, **13**, and **14**. Whether the Lord returns first or we are taken to heaven when we die, we want to be ready to appear before Him. Although His blood covers every flaw we possess, we do not want to feel ashamed. Peter stresses again and again the connection between our belief and our behavior.

Spotless and Blameless (verses 14–15a)

14 Wherefore, beloved, seeing that ye look for such things, be diligent that ye may be found of him in peace, without spot, and blameless. 15 And account that the longsuffering of our Lord is salvation;

The underlying theme of these verses is the second coming of the Lord. Whether our lives on Earth end in death or whether we are alive when the Lord returns, we want to be found ready. To be found "without spot, and blameless" is to be fully like Jesus (**verse 14**). This thought should motivate us to examine every aspect of our lives and think about how we would feel doing such and such when we are suddenly taken to be with the Lord. The standard is perfection, but the Lord knows our weaknesses and frailties, and the blood of Christ covers all of our sins. So we have great peace as we look forward to His return. The only reason the Lord is delaying His return is to give more people the opportunity to be saved before He comes back.

QUESTION 4

Write the three things Peter wants the "beloved" to have in Jesus.

"ye may be found of him in peace, without spot, and blameless."

LIGHT ON THE WORD

Ignoring Jesus' Return

Many people in our society live according to a "bumper sticker" mentality. Some believe they should "live fast, die young, and make a beautiful corpse." Others believe that "the person who dies with the most toys wins." These people live for immediate pleasure and are not concerned with the consequences. They believe they will somehow escape the consequences of their actions today and in the hereafter. They are either ignorant of or flatly denying the return of Christ and God's judgment of the rebellious.

BIBLE APPLICATION

AIM: That your students will remember that only God keeps every one of His promises.

A Promise Confirmed

A promise is a binding declaration between two or more people or institutions. Only God keeps every one of His promises. In this week's lesson, Peter confirms Christ's promise to return and usher in the new heaven and new earth.

STUDENTS' RESPONSE

AIM: That your students will understand how Peter's confirmation of Christ's promise to return and usher in the new heaven and new earth applies to us today.

Read the following Scripture texts. Identify the statements which are said to be the will of God: **1 Thessalonians 4:3; 5:18; 2 Peter 3:9.** Determine to obey God's will in these matters, until Jesus comes for you.

PRAYER

Dear God, You are a true promise keeper! Your Word is precious and holy to us and for us. We believe and trust that Jesus is coming back for His children. We wait with great joy and anticipation that He will return, and we will come back with Him. Bless You and Praise You! In Jesus' name, we pray.

DIG A LITTLE DEEPER

Although "the Day of the Lord," will be the greatest event the world will ever see, it rarely comes up on social media or radio talk-shows. Christians continue to pray, "Thy kingdom come. Thy will be done in earth, as it is in heaven" (Matthew 6:9-13, KJV) too often not appreciating its significance or anticipating the new heaven and a new earth it will usher in when there will be no more sorrow, pain, or death (Rev. 21:1, 4, KJV). Since hope is the anticipation of good, why does our anticipation of the ultimate good, "the Day of the Lord," seem to be at such a low level?

Forbes magazine reported a 12% increase in the number of people traveling to visit family and friends in 2021. There was a related increase in the numbers hopefully anticipating their visits.

Perhaps that was because there is a definite date for Thanksgiving, but there is also a definite end. There is no end to God's kingdom. How can Christians sustain their hope for "the Day of the Lord" without having any firm commitment as to when the "guests" will arrive? Jesus provided answers during His ministry on earth when he used the parables such as the one about the ten virgins keeping their oil ready to light their lamps (Matthew 25: 1-13).

More directly, in a vision John recorded in the Book of Revelation, Jesus admonished the church in Sardis, a "dead" church, to wake up, perfect themselves, and "hold fast and repent" or else "I will come on thee as a thief" because he had not "found thy works perfect before God" (Revelation 3:1-3, KJV). In contrast, He commended the church in Philadelphia for keeping His Word and advised them to "hold that fast which thou hast, that no man take thy crown" (Revelation 3:11, KJV). If Jesus returned today, what would he say to our churches and to each of us as individuals? Have we succumbed to sin like those in Sardis; have we become "lukewarm" like the church at Laodicea? (Revelation 3:14-15). Or are we obeying His command to persevere by patiently enduring temptation? (Revelation 3:10 KJV and *The Amplified Bible*).

HOW TO SAY IT

Perdition.	per-DIH-shun.
Scoffers.	SCOF-fers.

DAILY HOME BIBLE READINGS

MONDAY
Distressing Times Will Come
(2 Timothy 3:1–9)

TUESDAY
Warnings for False Prophets
(Jeremiah 23:23–32)

WEDNESDAY
Warnings for Rich Oppressors
(James 5:1–6)

THURSDAY
Return to the Lord
(Hosea 14:1-7)

FRIDAY
Teaching the Ways of God
(Micah 4:1-5)

SATURDAY
I Will Come Again
(John 14:1-7)

SUNDAY
The Promise of the Lord's Coming
(2 Peter 3:3-15a)

PREPARE FOR NEXT SUNDAY

Read **Isaiah 6:1–8,** and study "Holy, Holy, Holy."

Sources:
Green, Michael. Second Epistle General of Peter, and the General Epistle of Jude. Grand Rapids, MI: Eerdmans, 1987.
Lucas, Richard C., and Christopher Green. The Message of 2 Peter and Jude: The Promise of His Coming. Downers Grove, IL: InterVarsity, 1995.
Merriam-Webster Online Dictionary. http://www.merriam- webster.com (accessed November 3, 2011).
Mounce, Robert. A Living Hope: A Commentary on 1 and 2 Peter. Grand Rapids, MI: Eerdmans, 1982.
New Testament Greek Lexicon. http://www.biblestu- dytools.com/lexicons/greek (accessed October 31, 2011).
Zodhiates, Spiros. Complete Word Study Dictionary: New Testament. Iowa Falls, IA: World Bible Publishers, 1992. 710, 1487-1488.

COMMENTS / NOTES:

ANSWERS TO THE QUARTERLY QUIZ

LESSON 1

1. His garment was white as snow, and the hair of his head like pure wool: his throne was like the fiery flame, and his wheels as burning fire; 2. The beast was slain, and his body destroyed, and given to the burning flame.

LESSON 2

1. We have sinned, and have committed iniquity, and have done wickedly, and have rebelled, even by departing from thy precepts and from thy judgments: Neither have we hearkened unto thy servants the prophets, we have rebelled; 2. Righteousness, forgivenesses, mercies.

LESSON 3

1. Media and Persia; 2. Evening, morning, shut thou up.

LESSON 4

1. Paul makes the second comparison of believers as children of day; 2. God has chosen us for salvation through our Lord Jesus Christ.

LESSON 5

1. Kingdom of God; 2. Cup, blood, shed.

LESSON 6

1. Cleopas; 2. Their hearts burned within.

LESSON 7

1. He told them to touch (handle Him), showed them (his hands and feet), and ate (piece of fish on a honeycomb); 2. To Jerusalem and the temple.

LESSON 8

1. filled, speak with other tongues, utterance; 2. The wonderful works of God.

LESSON 9

1. The man who comes after Satan; 2. Paul states to hold to the traditions that have been taught, whether by word, or our epistle.

LESSON 10

1. Faith is the beginning of salvation; 2. Joy unspeakable.

LESSON 11

1. Precious promises; 2. blind; old sins.

LESSON 12

1. Answers may vary from having the same way of thinking to what approach is taken; 2. Answers may vary from all listed to selected ones, e.g., be sober and prayer.

LESSON 13

1. "Knowing this first, that there shall come in the last days scoffers, walking after their own lusts, And saying, Where is the promise of his coming? for since the fathers fell asleep, all things continue as they were from the beginning of the creation";

2. "The Lord is not slack concerning his promise, as some men count slackness; but is longsuffering to us- ward, not willing that any should perish, but that all should come to repentance."

The Symbol of the Church Of God In Christ

The Symbol of the Church Of God In Christ is an outgrowth of the Presiding Bishop's Coat of Arms, which has become quite familiar to the Church. The design of the Official Seal of the Church was created in 1973 and adopted in the General Assembly in 1981 (July Session).

The obvious GARNERED WHEAT in the center of the seal represents all of the people of the Church Of God In Christ, Inc. The ROPE of wheat that holds the shaft together represents the Founding Father of the Church, Bishop Charles Harrison Mason, who, at the call of the Lord, banded us together as a Brotherhood of Churches in the First Pentecostal General Assembly of the Church, in 1907.

The date in the seal has a two-fold purpose: first, to tell us that Bishop Mason received the baptism of the Holy Ghost in March 1907 and, second, to tell us that it was because of this outpouring that Bishop Mason was compelled to call us together in February of 1907 to organize the Church Of God In Christ.

The RAIN in the background represents the Latter Rain, or the End-time Revivals, which brought about the emergence of our Church along with other Pentecostal Holiness Bodies in 'he same era. The rain also serves as a challenge to the Church to keep Christ in the center of our worship and service, so that He may continue to use the Church Of God In Christ as one of the vehicles of Pentecostal Revival before the return of the Lord.

This information was reprinted from the book *So You Want to KNOW YOUR CHURCH* by Alferd Z. Hall, Jr.

COGIC AFFIRMATION OF FAITH

We believe the Bible to be the inspired and only infallible written Word of God.

We believe that there is One God, eternally existent in three Persons: God the Father, God the Son, and God the Holy Spirit.

We believe in the Blessed Hope, which is the rapture of the Church of God, which is in Christ at His return.

We believe that the only means of being cleansed from sin is through repentance and faith in the precious Blood of Jesus Christ.

We believe that regeneration by the Holy Ghost is absolutely essential for personal salvation.

We believe that the redemptive work of Christ on the Cross provides healing for the human body in answer to believing in prayer.

We believe that the baptism in the Holy Ghost, according to Acts 2:4, is given to believers who ask for it.

We believe in the sanctifying power of the Holy Spirit, by whose indwelling the Christian is enabled to live a Holy and separated life in this present world. Amen.

The Doctrines of the Church Of God In Christ

THE BIBLE

We believe that the Bible is the Word of God and contains one harmonious and sufficiently complete system of doctrine. We believe in the full inspiration of the Word of God. We hold the Word of God to be the only authority in all matters and assert that no doctrine can be true or essential if it does not find a place in this Word.

THE FATHER

We believe in God, the Father Almighty, the Author and Creator of all things. The Old Testament reveals God in diverse manners, by manifesting His nature, character, and dominions. The Gospels in the New Testament give us knowledge of God the "Father" or "My Father," showing the relationship of God to Jesus as Father, or representing Him as the Father in the Godhead, and Jesus himself that Son (St. John 15:8, 14:20). Jesus also gives God the distinction of "Fatherhood" to all believers when He explains God in the light of "Your Father in Heaven" (St. Matthew 6:8).

THE SON

We believe that Jesus Christ is the Son of God, the second person in the Godhead of the Trinity or Triune Godhead. We believe that Jesus was and is eternal in His person and nature as the Son of God who was with God in the beginning of creation (St. John 1:1). We believe that Jesus Christ was born of a virgin called Mary according to the Scripture (St. Matthew 1:18), thus giving rise to our fundamental belief in the Virgin

Birth and to all of the miraculous events surrounding the phenomenon (St. Matthew 1:18–25). We believe that Jesus Christ became the "suffering servant" to man; this suffering servant came seeking to redeem man from sin and to reconcile him to God, his Father (Romans 5:10). We believe that Jesus Christ is standing now as mediator between God and man (I Timothy 2:5).

THE HOLY GHOST

We believe the Holy Ghost or Holy Spirit is the third person of the Trinity; proceeds from the Father and the Son; is of the same substance, equal to power and glory; and is together with the Father and the Son, to be believed in, obeyed, and worshiped. The Holy Ghost is a gift bestowed upon the believer for the purpose of equipping and empowering the believer, making him or her a more effective witness for service in the world. He teaches and guides one into all truth (John 16:13; Acts 1:8, 8:39).

THE BAPTISM OF THE HOLY GHOST

We believe that the Baptism of the Holy Ghost is an experience subsequent to conversion and sanctification and that tongue-speaking is the consequence of the baptism in the Holy Ghost with the manifestations of the fruit of the spirit (Galatians 5:22–23; Acts 10:46, 19:1–6). We believe that we are not baptized with the Holy Ghost in order to be saved (Acts 19:1–6; John 3:5). When one receives a baptismal Holy Ghost experience, we believe one will speak with a tongue unknown to oneself according to the sovereign will of Christ. To be filled with the Spirit means to be Spirit controlled as expressed by Paul in Ephesians 5:18,19. Since the charismatic demonstrations were necessary to help the early church to be successful in implementing the command of Christ, we, therefore, believe that a Holy Ghost experience is mandatory for all believers today.

MAN

We believe that humankind was created holy by God, composed of body, soul, and spirit. We believe that humankind, by nature, is sinful and unholy. Being born in sin, a person needs to be born again, sanctified and cleansed from all sins by the blood of Jesus. We believe that one is saved by confessing and forsaking one's sins, and believing on the Lord Jesus Christ, and that having become a child of God, by being born again and adopted into the family of God, one may, and should, claim the inheritance of the sons of God, namely the baptism of the Holy Ghost.

SIN

Sin, the Bible teaches, began in the angelic world (Ezekiel 28:11–19; Isaiah 14:12–20) and is transmitted into the blood of the human race through disobedience and deception motivated by unbelief (I Timothy 2:14). Adam's sin, committed by eating of the forbidden fruit from the tree of knowledge of good and evil, carried with it permanent pollution or depraved human nature to all his descendants. This is called "original sin." Sin

can now be defined as a volitional transgression against God and a lack of conformity to the will of God. We, therefore, conclude that humankind by nature is sinful and has fallen from a glorious and righteous state from which we were created, and has become unrighteous and unholy. We therefore, must be restored to the state of holiness from which we have fallen by being born again (St. John 3:7).

SALVATION

Salvation deals with the application of the work of redemption to the sinner with restoration to divine favor and communion with God. This redemptive operation of the Holy Ghost upon sinners is brought about by repentance toward God and faith toward our Lord Jesus Christ which brings conversion, faith, justification, regeneration, sanctification, and the baptism of the Holy Ghost. Repentance is the work of God, which results in a change of mind in respect to a person's relationship to God (St. Matthew 3:1–2, 4:17; Acts 20:21). Faith is a certain conviction wrought in the heart by the Holy Spirit, as to the truth of the Gospel and a heart trust in the promises of God in Christ (Romans 1:17, 3:28; St. Matthew 9:22; Acts 26:18). Conversion is that act of God whereby He causes the regenerated sinner, in one's conscious life, to turn to Him in repentance and faith (II Kings 5:15; II Chronicles 33:12,13; St. Luke 19:8,9; Acts 8:30). Regeneration is the act of God by which the principle of the new life is implanted in humankind, the governing disposition of soul is made holy, and the first holy exercise of this new disposition is secured. Sanctification is that gracious and continuous operation of the Holy Ghost, by which He delivers the justified sinner from the pollution of sin, renews a person's whole nature in the image of God, and enables one to perform good works (Romans 6:4, 5:6; Colossians 2:12, 3:1).

ANGELS

The Bible uses the term "angel" (a heavenly body) clearly and primarily to denote messengers or ambassadors of God with such Scripture references as Revelations 4:5, which indicates their duty in heaven to praise God (Psalm 103:20), to do God's will (St. Matthew 18:10), and to behold His face. But since heaven must come down to earth, they also have a mission to earth. The Bible indicates that they accompanied God in the Creation, and also that they will accompany Christ in His return in Glory.

DEMONS

Demons denote unclean or evil spirits; they are sometimes called devils or demonic beings. They are evil spirits, belonging to the unseen or spiritual realm, embodied in human beings. The Old Testament refers to the prince of demons, sometimes called Satan (adversary) or Devil, as having power and wisdom, taking the habitation of other forms such as the serpent (Genesis 3:1). The New Testament speaks of the Devil as Tempter (St. Matthew 4:3), and it goes on to tell the works of

Satan, the Devil, and demons as combating righteousness and good in any form, proving to be an adversary to the saints. Their chief power is exercised to destroy the mission of Jesus Christ. It can well be said that the Christian Church believes in demons, Satan, and devils. We believe in their power and purpose. We believe they can be subdued and conquered as in the commandment to the believer by Jesus. "In my name they shall cast out Satan and the work of the Devil and to resist him and then he will flee (WITHDRAW) from you" (St. Mark 16:17).

THE CHURCH

The Church forms a spiritual unity of which Christ is the divine head. It is animated by one Spirit, the Spirit of Christ. It professes one faith, shares one hope, and serves one King. It is the citadel of the truth and God's agency for communicating to believers all spiritual blessings. The Church then is the object of our faith rather than of knowledge. The name of our Church, "CHURCH OF GOD IN CHRIST," is supported by I Thessalonians 2:14 and other passages in the Pauline Epistles. The word "CHURCH" or "EKKLESIA" was first applied to the Christian society by Jesus Christ in St. Matthew 16:18, the occasion being that of His benediction of Peter at Caesarea Philippi.

THE SECOND COMING OF CHRIST

We believe in the second coming of Christ; that He shall come from heaven to earth, personally, bodily, visibly (Acts 1:11; Titus 2:11–13; St. Matthew 16:27, 24:30, 25:30; Luke 21:27; John 1:14, 17; Titus 2:11); and that the Church, the bride, will be caught up to meet Him in the air (I Thessalonians 4:16–17). We admonish all who have this hope to purify themselves as He is pure.

DIVINE HEALING

The Church Of God In Christ believes in and practices Divine Healing. It is a commandment of Jesus to the Apostles (St. Mark 16:18). Jesus affirms His teachings on healing by explaining to His disciples, who were to be Apostles, that healing the afflicted is by faith (St. Luke 9:40–41). Therefore, we believe that healing by faith in God has scriptural support and ordained authority. St. James's writings in his epistle encourage Elders to pray for the sick, lay hands upon them and to anoint them with oil, and state that prayers with faith shall heal the sick and the Lord shall raise them up. Healing is still practiced widely and frequently in the Church Of God In Christ, and testimonies of healing in our Church testify to this fact.

MIRACLES

The Church Of God In Christ believes that miracles occur to convince people that the Bible is God's Word. A miracle can be defined as an extraordinary visible act of divine power, wrought by the efficient agency of the will of God, which has as its final cause the vindication of the righteousness of God's Word. We believe that the works of God, which were performed during the beginnings of Christianity, do and will occur even today where God is preached, faith in Christ is exercised, the Holy Ghost is active, and the Gospel is promulgated in the truth (Acts 5:15, 6:8, 9:40; Luke 4:36, 7:14, 15, 5:5, 6; St. Mark 14:15).

THE ORDINANCES OF THE CHURCH

It is generally admitted that for an ordinance to be valid, it must have been instituted by Christ. When we speak of ordinances of the church, we are speaking of those instituted by Christ, in which by sensible signs the grace of God in Christ and the benefits of the covenant of grace are represented, sealed, and applied to believers, and these in turn give expression to their faith and allegiance to God. The Church Of God In Christ recognizes three ordinances as having been instituted by Christ himself and, therefore, are binding upon the church practice.

THE LORD'S SUPPER (HOLY COMMUNION)

The Lord's Supper symbolizes the Lord's death and suffering for the benefit and in the place of His people. It also symbolizes the believer's participation in the crucified Christ. It represents not only the death of Christ as the object of faith, which unites the believers to Christ, but also the effect of this act as the giving of life, strength, and joy to the soul. The communicant by faith enters into a special spiritual union of one's soul with the glorified Christ.

FOOT WASHING

Foot washing is practiced and recognized as an ordinance in our Church because Christ, by His example, showed that humility characterized greatness in the kingdom of God, and that service rendered to others gave evidence that humility, motivated by love, exists. These services are held subsequent to the Lord's Supper; however, its regularity is left to the discretion of the pastor in charge.

WATER BAPTISM

We believe that Water Baptism is necessary as instructed by Christ in St. John 3:5, "UNLESS MAN BE BORN AGAIN OF WATER AND OF THE SPIRIT..."

However, we do not believe that water baptism alone is a means of salvation, but is an outward demonstration that one has already had a conversion experience and has accepted Christ as his personal Savior. As Pentecostals, we practice immersion in preference to sprinkling because immersion corresponds more closely to the death, burial, and resurrection of our Lord (Colossians 2:12). It also symbolizes regeneration and purification more than any other mode. Therefore, we practice immersion as our mode of baptism. We believe that we should use the Baptismal Formula given to us by Christ for all "...IN THE NAME OF THE FATHER, AND OF THE SON, AND OF THE HOLY GHOST..." (Matthew 28:19).

SUGGESTED ORDER OF SERVICE

1. Call to order.
2. Singing.
3. Prayer.
4. Responsive reading:

Supt.: Behold, how good and how pleasant it is for brethren to dwell together in unity!

Psalm 133:1

School: And let the peace of God rule in your hearts, to the which also ye are called in one body; and be ye thankful.

Colossians 3:15

Supt.: Blessed are they that dwell in thy house: they will be still praising thee.

Psalm 84:4

School: Praise ye the LORD. I will praise the LORD with my whole heart, in the assembly of the upright, and in the congregation.

Psalm 111:1

Supt.: And the LORD said unto him, I have heard thy prayer and thy supplication, that thou hast made before me: I have hallowed this house, which thou hast built, to put my name there for ever; and mine eyes and mine heart shall be there perpetually.

1 Kings 9:3

School: Ye shall keep my sabbaths, and reverence my sanctuary: I am the LORD.

Leviticus 19:30

Supt.: And I say also unto thee, That thou art Peter, and upon this rock I will build my church; and the gates of hell shall not prevail against it.

Matthew 16:18

School: My soul longeth, yea, even fainteth for the courts of the LORD: my heart and my flesh crieth out for the living God.

Psalm 84:2

Supt.: And other sheep I have, which are not of this fold: them also I must bring, and they shall hear my voice; and there shall be one fold, and one shepherd.

John 10:16

School: But if I tarry long, that thou mayest know how thou oughtest to behave thyself in the house of God, which is the church of the living God, the pillar and ground of the truth.

1 Timothy 3:15

All: Lift up your hands in the sanctuary, and bless the LORD.

Psalm 134:2

5. Singing.
6. Reading lesson by school and superintendent.
7. Classes assemble for lesson study.
8. Sunday School offering.
9. Five-minute warning bell.
10. Closing bell.
11. Brief lesson review by pastor or superintendent.
12. Secretary's report.
13. Announcements.
14. Dismissal.